Teaching in a Chromebook Classroom

Dr. Barbara Sweet, Ed.D.

Teaching in a Chromebook Classroom

DEDICATION

I dedicate this book to my husband, son, and mom for their unwavering support and encouragement. I also dedicate this book to all the students I have ever taught, and all the students I have yet to teach. I learn as much from you, as you learn from me. Go out there and make me proud!

CONTENTS

INTRODUCTION

When I was in elementary school, I took a computer class. It met once or twice a week. We went to the computer lab. The lab consisted of a room with computers lining the walls. The computers were big and white. The monitor of the computer was as big as a large cardboard box. The computer screen was dark, almost black. The cursor was a small green rectangular box that blinked on the screen. We had to quietly sit in front of the computer and wait for the computer teacher to make her way around. When she arrived to my computer, she inserted a large floppy disk into it. She then hit a series of F key functions and started a Math problem program. I was to answer the Math questions and click on next once I had answered it. At the end of the program, I would raise my hand and the teacher would come over and write something down. I now guess that she was given a summary of my score and she was keeping track of my understanding of the material.

I remember looking forward to my computer class. I even got a sticker one day that said, "Computer Whiz." Now reflecting back on that experience, I never actually learned anything new from my computer class. I only practiced what I had already learned in class. I also did not work on anything other than Math. For a while I wondered if computers were used only for Math because that seemed to be all I did with it.

At the beginning of my college years, I took a psychology class. I had an electric typewriter at home. My mom was a secretary from the typewriter years. Even though computers were available at that time, we couldn't afford one. My psychology professor gave us an assignment that was worth a lot of points. She said it had to be done on a computer. At the end of class I spoke to her and told her that I did not have a computer at home. I asked if I could type the assignment on my typewriter. Her response I would never forget. She said, "You are living in the era of the computer, not the typewriter. You either write it on a computer or I'll flunk you." However harsh her response was, it was important for me to hear. I could not rely on what was comfortable and known. I had to go outside of my comfort zone and learn how to use a computer. I spent long hours at the university's library learning how to use the computer and learning how to type my assignments. I remember one of the first programs I worked on was Microsoft PowerPoint. The librarian assistant was very patient with me. I would try something, think I messed it up, raise my hand, and he would come over and ask me what I was trying to do and tell me how to do it correctly. I'm appreciative of his kindness, without it I wouldn't have overcome such a scary and intimidating challenge.

I remember a world without Internet, cell phones, and online games. I remember how hard it was to transition from a regular cell phone (dumb phone) to a smartphone. All of those things were scary and intimidating initially, but I eventually adapted and now I can't live without those things.

I'm a Spanish teacher and technology lead at my school. My

graduate degrees are in educational technology. I am passionate about education and the use of technology in education. In this book I narrate my journey with technology, I share my experiences as the technology lead of a 1:1 school, and I also include suggestions and tips for any teacher or administrator considering implementing technology in the classroom. I wrote this book as a way to help my fellow teachers adapt to changing times. I understand that it can be hard trying to teach with a Chromebook when you might have never seen one before, but you can do it!

1 A CHROMEBOOK ISN'T A PC, IT'S BETTER

When I first heard of a Chromebook, I thought, "You get what you pay for. There's no way a computer that cheap can be any good. It must be disposable. Maybe you use it for a year and then replace it." However, when my school became a Google School and I was asked to lead the technology implementation, I thought, "Okay, this is an opportunity to learn something new." My school had no technology prior to this, so any type of technology in my mind was a blessing.

As the technology lead at my school, I was in charge of training the students on how to use the Chromebooks and troubleshoot any problems. I shared these duties initially with another very talented teacher, who without her help, I wouldn't have been able to have survived this process. Teachers were given very minimal training from the school district, which also meant helping them better serve the students. We first rolled out Chromebooks to 10th and 11th graders in March. That meant approximately 800 students received Chromebooks. The day of the rollout my principal got a substitute teacher to cover my classes and I was to go around from class to class and help the teachers and students get set-up with their Chromebooks.

We focused on English and Social Science classes on the first roll-out because those teachers worked with all the students in those grade levels, whereas other subjects would have a mixture of grade levels and this would have made the roll-out even more complicated. We started with 11th grade English classes and 3 weeks later did 10th grade Social Studies classes.

Day 1 was very stressful to say the least. Students had a lot of questions and we didn't necessarily know all the answers. The district provided a scripted lesson as a guide for teachers. Those who felt comfortable enough to venture beyond the scripted lesson, did so, and the ones that were not as comfortable with technology, followed the lesson plan.

Some teachers struggled to keep everyone on task. The students who were tech savvy completed the tasks quickly and went on to explore what else they could do with their new Chromebook. The students who had never had a computer before, let alone a Chromebook, were apprehensive and needed to be guided step-by-step and reassured that they were doing things correctly.

The personalities of the teachers influenced the success of their lessons as well. The "control freaks" were overly stressed about any movement the students made without been given specific instructions. The teacher with no real behavior management plan before the Chromebooks, had some students listening and following, others lost, others doing other things who then didn't know what the next step was in the lesson. One teacher modified the lesson to include material specific to her class. They had been working on supporting claims or arguments, so they were asked to give an opinion on a specific topic, provide a quote to support their claim, and cite the quote correctly using MLA in Google Classroom. They were then to comment on what their peers had written. This was both good and bad.

Students had not been given the chance to just play with the commenting capabilities nor had they ever seen

Google Classroom before. Students quickly posted comments that were irrelevant or inappropriate. Because we had never taught a lesson like this before, we didn't realize how a lesson could quickly get out of hand. Another teacher shared a Google Doc she created with all the students in the class, giving everyone editing rights. That also turned into chaos. This time students weren't only posting inappropriate comments, they were also adding inappropriate images, and deleting the work of others. We had never implemented Chromebooks like this before, so we were learning as we went.

I quickly learned that Chromebooks have very little local memory. Everything is saved on the cloud and not on the device. At first that worried me. How can I trust that the work I've spent hours writing is somewhere in the cloud? What if it gets deleted somehow? It turned out that the fact the data was stored in the cloud and not on the device itself was a good thing. It meant that when I opened the

Chromebook, it was ready to go within seconds. That's something my pc couldn't do.

It also worked as a single sign-on. Students signed on with their school Gmail accounts and were automatically logged-in to everything the Chromebook had to offer. At first, students struggled with just being able to log-in to their Chromebooks. The email provided by the district was unnecessarily complicated. The email address included the student's first initial, last name first initial, their student ID backwards, and another number at the end. Students were told to change their passwords and write them down on a paper for the teacher as well as provide it to the district via a Google Form. Websites that required a separate sign on, offered the student the ability to sign in using their Google account, which made the process much quicker and easier to remember all the passwords.

Downloads were different. I was used to having to download programs to my computer in order for it to work properly, usually in the form of plug-ins. With Chrome, the

Google browser, downloads were redesigned as extensions, add-ons, and apps that didn't download unnecessary files on the device, but instead resided on the browser.

The keyboard was similar, but had some keys missing and some additional ones. The kids quickly asked, "How do you right click?" I said, like you always do. They said, "No, that doesn't work." I then learned that in order to right click you need to use two fingers and double tap the touchpad, similar to what you would do on a Mac. Of course that conversation was followed by asking, "What do all those keys do?" To which I answered, "I don't know, but I guess we're going to find out."

Chromebook Keyboard Keys

Hold this key down along with Ctrl to take a screenshot.

Hold this key along with Ctrl to mirror the screen on your Chromebook to a projector.

The search button allows you to search for apps and information on the web.

For Delete, use the backspace key or Alt + backspace.

There are other special keys, but I found these to be the least intuitive to figure out and the ones I use the most. If you're wondering what the other ones do, you can press Ctrl + alt+ / and it will show you on the screen what the combination of keys can do. After a few days, students found it fun to find new shortcut keys for their Chromebooks and teach one another new tricks.

Within Gmail or the Drive, you will find what people refer to as "the waffle" or tic-tac-toe board.

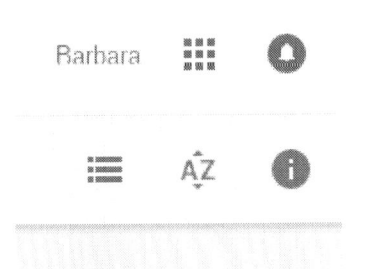

In some Chromebooks you will see it on the bottom left corner of the screen. The waffle allows you to switch between programs. For example, you're writing an email and you want to open another tab and start a Google Slide, click on the waffle.

2 CHROMEBOOK SCHOOL

In order for a school to be classified as a Google for Education school, the school district needs to register the district as a Google Apps for Education (GAFE) school district. Once this has happened, each of the schools will be provided access for creating Gmail accounts for the students. These email accounts are special because it identifies the student as being part of GAFE. While most Google tools are open to anyone with a Gmail account, some are limited to GAFE schools, like Google Classroom. It's then up to the school district to decide what access or limits each school and teacher will have within the Google domain.

Being a Chromebook school means that students are using Chromebooks to access the Internet and are relying on GAFE to conduct their day-to-day activities. Being a 1:1 school means that every student has their own Chromebook. Some schools use a cart model where the Chromebook stays at school, and others check-out the Chromebook to the student and he/she takes it home every day and brings it back, as they would do with their textbooks. Both methods have pros and cons.

For example, students need to be able to remember their Gmail account and password. Without this, they will not be able to log-in to their Chromebook. We developed a back-up plan for this. We had all students fill out a Google Form with their password information. Each teacher wrote down the passwords for their class. Lastly, one person on site was given authority to re-set passwords if needed.

Our district chose to allow students to take their Chromebooks home and bring them to school. This meant that I had students who left their Chromebook at home or forgot to charge it. These students got to work with a partner for the day and hopefully this was enough to motivate them to remember to bring it to class the next day. Some parents chose for their child not to use a Chromebook at all. They didn't want to be liable for it. The district provided the parents with the option of getting insurance for their Chromebook. However, the details on the insurance were not clear to the students and there was confusion as to how to get the insurance and file a claim. Students also expressed fear of mishandling the Chromebook as they were suddenly responsible for a $400 piece of equipment.

I had a high school junior who didn't know how to email. I had others who had never had a computer of their own. Providing each student with the same device allowed equality among the students. There was no longer a digital divide among those who had the tech skills because they could afford it and those who couldn't. However, that did mean that I now not only needed to differentiate based on the student's level in my subject, but also based on their technology skills. The same proved to be true with the teachers. They were all starting from different points. Some with a lot of experience in technology and others, not so much.

While we were giving all students a Chromebook, we were not giving all students Internet access. Some students did not have Internet access at home. Luckily, GAFE allows students to do some work offline. Teachers learned that they needed to be careful when assigning due dates for assignments that required the use of the Internet beyond GAFE. Some teachers had never had the need of working offline on a Google Doc, so they did not know how to do it or how to teach the students how to do it. In hindsight, we should have taught both the teachers and students how to access their work offline in the initial training or in a subsequent training.

To enable offline access while you have an Internet connection, you can turn offline access on or off from your Google Drive or from within the menu in Docs, Sheets, or Slides.

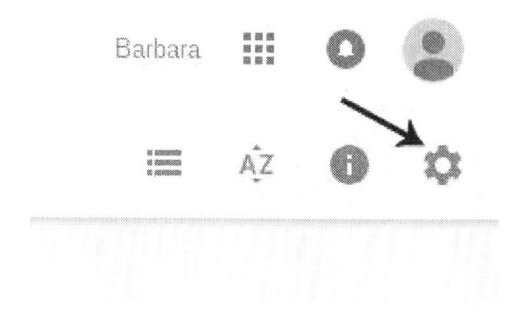

Once enabled, when you are offline you can open your saved documents and the edits will be saved offline. The work then automatically syncs when the Chromebook is again connected to the Internet. You can also download the Google Docs, Sheets, Slides, and Drive apps on your smartphone, then you can work offline from your phone as well. Add-ons and extensions will probably not work offline, but you will be able to use the basic Google programs. Be aware that if you worked collaboratively with another person on a document, once you connect to the Internet, some of those changes might override the other.

Being a 1:1 Chromebook school allowed us to become less dependent on paper. We realized that there was no longer the need to print worksheets or project instructions when we could easily share them online with the students and they would have access to it. It not only reduced the cost of printing and paper purchases, but it also taught our students to be green and more conscious of the planet. The Chromebooks were not set-up to allow printing, on purpose. We didn't want the students to accidently start printing documents to school remotely and we wanted to minimize the reliance on paper. Students who needed to print something would go to the school library and use one of the computers there to print. The school librarian helped me keep track of the students who were excessively printing in the library so I could then educate both the teacher and the students on how else to do the same assignment without the need of paper.

Students were able to collaborate and do group writing and publishing more easily. Everyone now had a device and instead of everyone taking turns working on the same document, they could work together on the same document, at the same time. This motivated students to contribute work to the group assignment and not rely on one person to do all the work.

Learning was also occurring 24/7; it was no longer limited to the bell. Students were independently choosing to continue course discussions and working on course assignments beyond the course time. Because of this, I've added the Gmail app to my cell phone. If they need to contact me after school hours, they can reach me. Students have commented that they like this. It shows them I care and that I am approachable.

3 GOOGLE APPS FOR EDUCATION (GAFE)

GAFE includes the basic Google tools: Google Docs (similar to Word), Google Sheets (similar to Excel), Google Slides (similar to PowerPoint), Google Sites, Drive, Gmail, Calendar, and now Google Classroom. If you were working on a pc, you would have to pay for the office suite package, which includes Word, Excel, and PowerPoint, but with GAFE, all of the Google programs are free.

Chromebooks come with many of these GAFE programs already installed. To find them, click on the magnifying glass on the bottom of the screen or on the waffle.

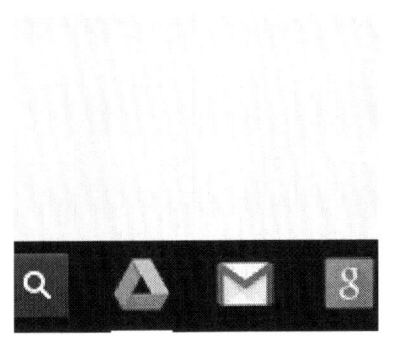

At our school, teachers are issued a pc and students are given Chromebooks. I realized that as a teacher, I was relying on my pc to do day-to-day tasks. If I had to create a document, I would open Microsoft Word. If I needed to make a presentation, I opened Microsoft PowerPoint. However, by doing this, I wasn't immersing myself in the Chromebook experience; I wasn't diving into using GAFE. I was relying on the programs that I knew really well and the ones I was most comfortable with. I realized that in order to truly understand my students and help them with their Chromebooks, I had to push myself to use a Chromebook for everything. I equate this to learning a second language. If you have the opportunity to immerse yourself in the language, do it. There will be no better learning experience.

I'll go over each of these programs briefly, as well as provide some ideas. I'll start with Google Docs.

Google Docs, like I mentioned earlier, is similar to Word. It's a processor program that allows you to type documents, insert tables, images, format letters, font size, etc.

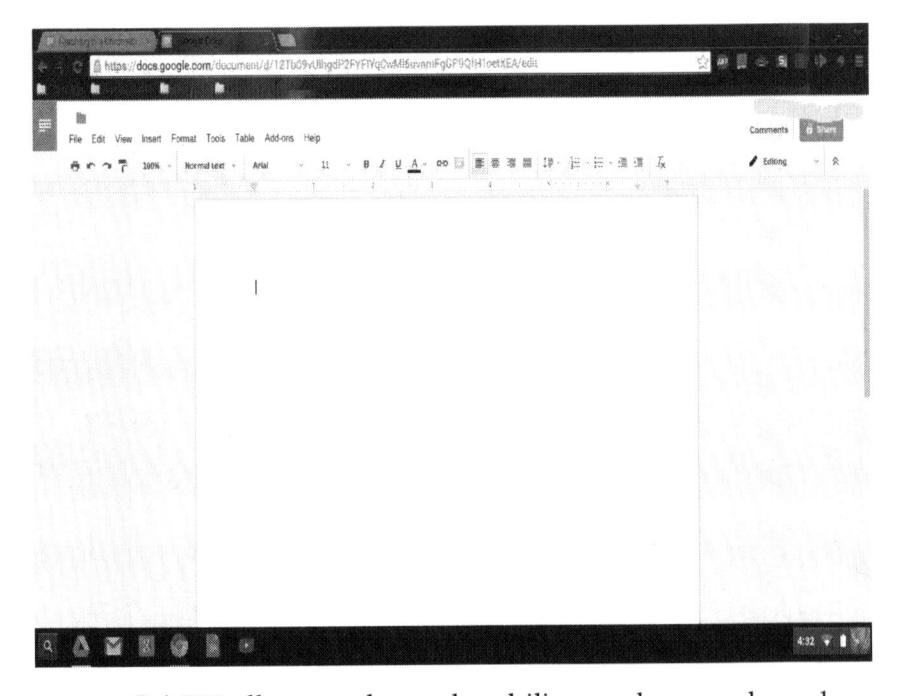

GAFE allow students the ability to share and work collaboratively on the same document. Instead of one person doing the work and the others staring at the screen, everyone can be engaged in the lesson. Teachers can also track the changes made to each document in the revision history. Press File, and then then pick the selection history. You can revert the document to a previous edition if you want. No more hitting "save as" to save each revision. All changes are saved on the cloud.

The share button allows you to choose the sharing privileges that you want to give others: can edit, can comment, or can view only. You would give can edit privileges to someone you want to allow the ability to make changes to the document; can comment if you don't want the person to actually change the text, but want them to suggest changes; and can view only allows the person to view the document and they cannot make any changes. Additionally, since GAFE is available online, students can access their work from anywhere and at any time. They don't need to be working on a Chromebook.

Google Sheets is a spreadsheet program. It allows you to tabulate data and generate charts or tables with the information. It's good for organizing information, planning, keeping track of lab results, etc.

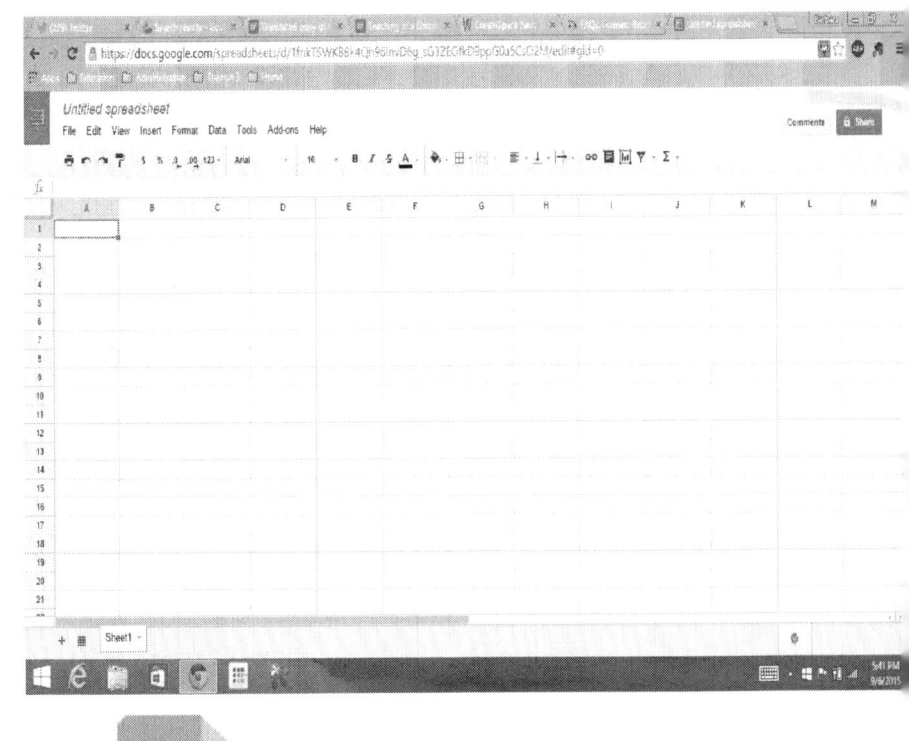

Google Slides is a presentation program. As the name indicates, it lets you create slides. You can change the theme, layout, transitions, color scheme, etc.

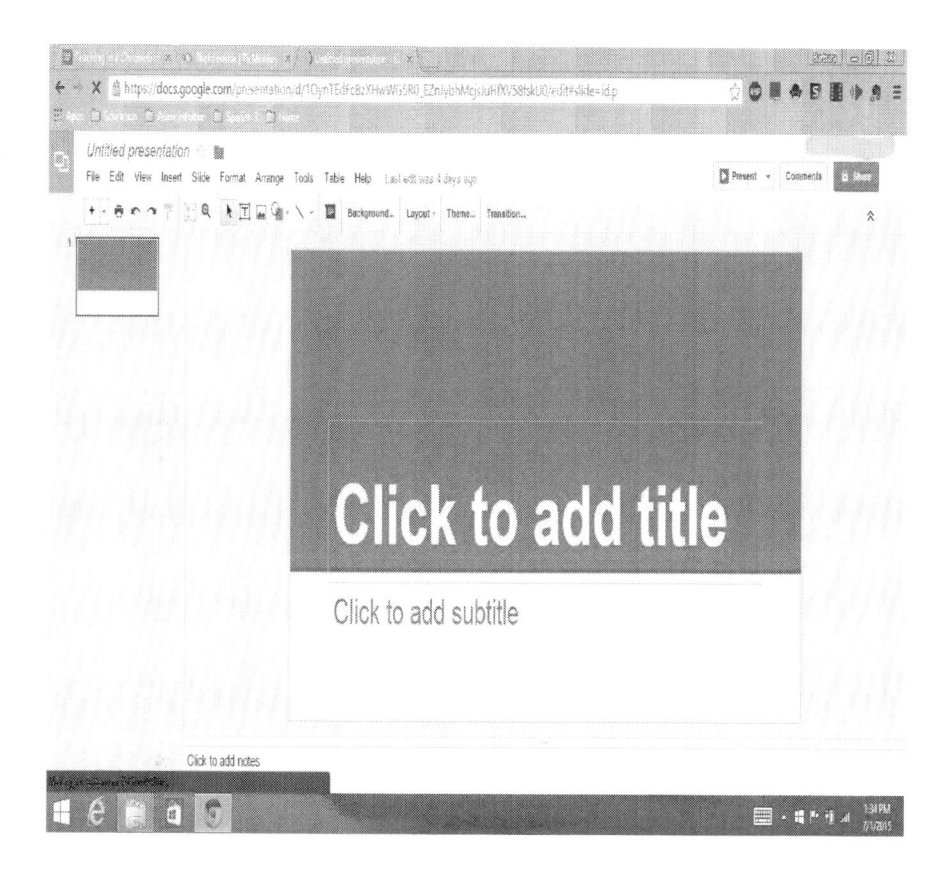

Use it to create lesson presentations, take notes, etc. I've given students a list of topics that were related to our lesson, then divided the students into small groups and they chose the topic for their group. I tell them what I want the presentation to include, such as the number of slides, graphics, data, etc. The students then divide the workload and work together on the assignment. The last thing we do is to have the groups present and explain their Google Slides to the class.

I'll share some of my experiences with Google Slides. First, I assigned students to small groups and had them to choose a topic to work together on, like I said above. One of the students in the group was absent the following day. The students in his group called me over, "Mrs. Sweet, you need to come see this." When I walked over and looked at the screen I saw the cursor moving and text was being written into the slide. I asked, "Who is writing?" They said, "It's Andrew." "But, I thought Andrew was sick." "He is, but he's doing his part from home". I smiled in amazement. I was speechless. Andrew, being the good student that he was, wanted to do his part of the work, even if he was sick, and GAFE allowed him to do just that. Now, I'm not saying that you should require all sick students to work from home, but for those go-getters in our classrooms, they have the option with Chromebook.

Here's another story. I often make PowerPoints for the grammar part of my lessons. I spent a few hours on a Sunday afternoon working on it. I made sure it made sense, was visually appealing, and easy for students to follow. I have a work computer and a home computer. When I did anything work related from home, I would email it to myself so that I would have it at school. Well, somehow I forgot to do that this time. I managed to get to school and the file I needed was safely stored on my pc at home. (Shhhhh, don't tell my principal.) Luckily, it was on a topic I knew really well and I could teach without the aid of a PowerPoint. Had I done the presentation using Google Slides, that wouldn't had happened. It would have been saved to the cloud and accessible from any computer. Needless to say, ever since I started using GAFE, that hasn't happened again!

Next on the list of GAFE is Google Sites. Google Sites is perhaps more complex than the rest of the programs. It allows you to create websites that are tied to the school's domain. You can control who can see it or make it public.

Google Sites is good for having students create their own webpages or having them create an e-portfolio to showcase their work.

 **Drive** is where everything is saved to. It's the equivalent of My Computer or My Documents files on your computer. Whenever you open or create something within GAFE, it is stored here. Created something and don't know where it went? It will be in your Drive. I suggest making folders and moving your documents into them. It will help you stay organized. Also, there's a Google search bar built into the Drive. You can use that to search by title or content of the document.

Gmail is the Google email. Some schools choose to have different setting on their email depending on the grade level. Maybe K-2 can only email the teacher, 3rd through 5th can email within the school, and 6th-12th can email anyone inside or outside the school. The Gmail account for Google districts comes ad free, which is great! No need to worry about an inappropriate ad showing up in their email or providing the students with an unnecessary distraction.

Google Calendar is just that, a calendar.

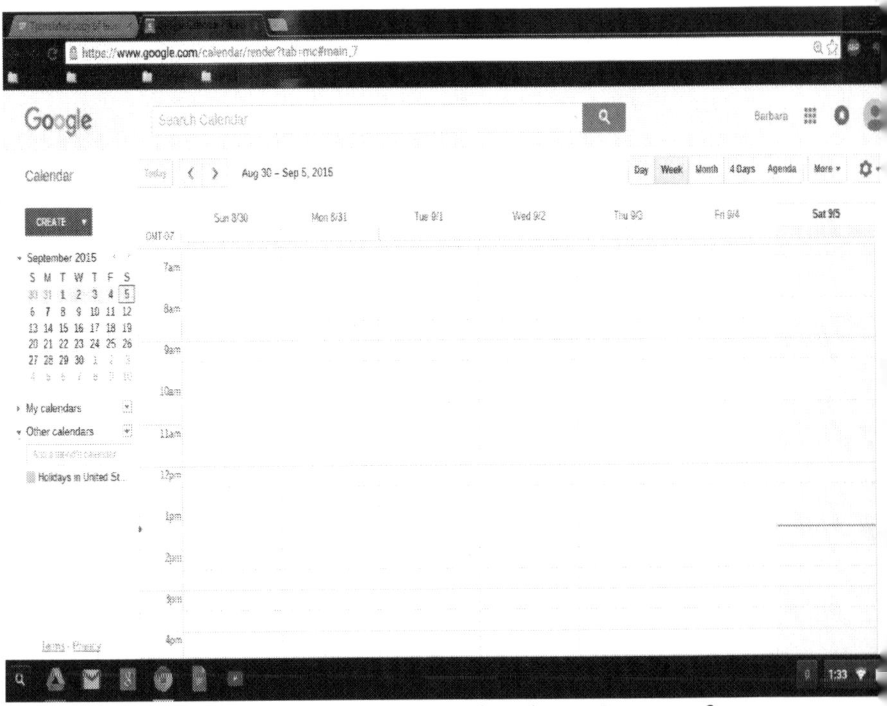

Students can have one or more calendars. Some of our students have a personal and a school calendar. Every year we buy and issue the students printed planners. We still do that, but we encourage them to use Google Calendar instead. I tell them to color code their classes and to set-up reminders for upcoming tests and quizzes. It helps students manage their time. Many of my students take AP classes, play at least one sport (if not more), and have after school jobs. Let's face it, they're not naturally organized. We need to teach them the skills that they will need to survive in the real world.

Google Classroom is the newest of the Google products. If you have ever taken an online course and used a learning management system (LMS) like Blackboard, this has a similar feel. However, it's not fully an LMS, it's more of an organizational tool.

Teachers create their class and either sign-up the students via email or provide them with the class code. Students register, put in the code, and have access to the class. Google Classroom automatically creates a folder in your Drive for each of your classes, so any work the student submits to his Science class, for example, will also be stored in the Science folder in his drive. The same is true for teachers.

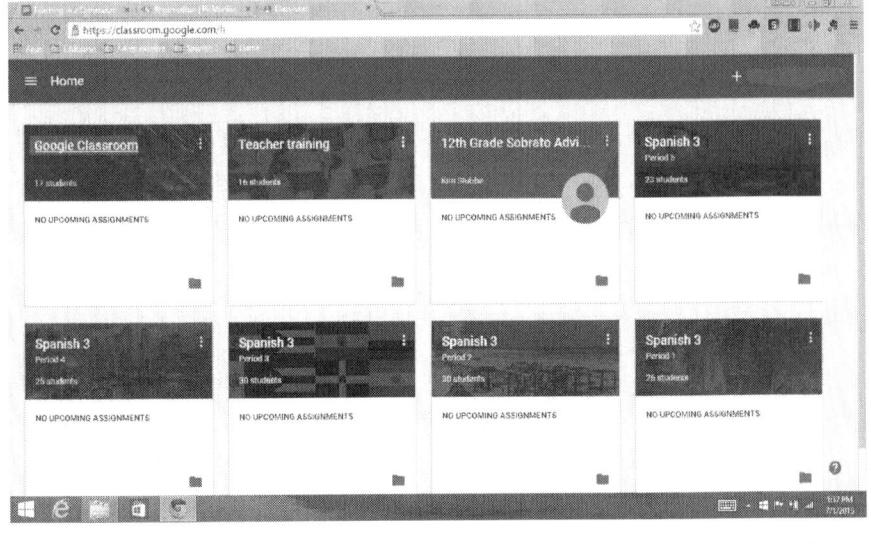

Inside the class, Google Classroom allows the teacher to create announcements and assignments. Google Classroom makes it easy for students to respond to assignments. Students click open next to the assignment and select how they wish to respond to the assignment, whether a Google Doc, Sheet, Slide, etc., then it automatically opens a new window. The new window will automatically put the name of the assignment and the name of the student. It used to drive me crazy when students handed in work without a name - this solves that problem.

Additionally, Google Classroom generates a turn-in button on the top right-hand corner of the page. When students have completed their work, they hit the turn-in button and off it goes. Google Classroom tells you how many students have submitted, how many are late, and how many are missing and who the students are.

It has three tabs at the top: **Stream, Students, and About**. The **stream** is where the announcements and assignments are posted. It scrolls downward as the page fills up, so the assignment on the top would be the most recent one. The **students** tab indicates what students are enrolled in the class and it allows you to email them from there as well. The **about** tab is where I suggest you put important information or something that the students will need to access often. For example, that's where I put the digital copy of their textbook. If your textbook is old like mine, it's probably out of copyright. You can scan the chapter that you're working on and upload that section to Google

Classroom. You can use the about section to put handouts, study guides, etc.

Grading in Google Classroom is a lot easier than carrying hundreds of essays back and forth and potentially losing one or two along the way. Google Classroom has an area for grading. It currently doesn't connect with any gradebook program; however, you can review the work online, assign it a grade, and then download the results as an Excel spreadsheet. I don't know why it doesn't turn it into a Google Sheet. You can input those grades into your online gradebook from the Excel spreadsheet. Sometimes I just put a 1 or a 0 for grading. A 1 tells me the student presented the work in front of the class and 0 that they haven't. I then put the actual points in the gradebook.

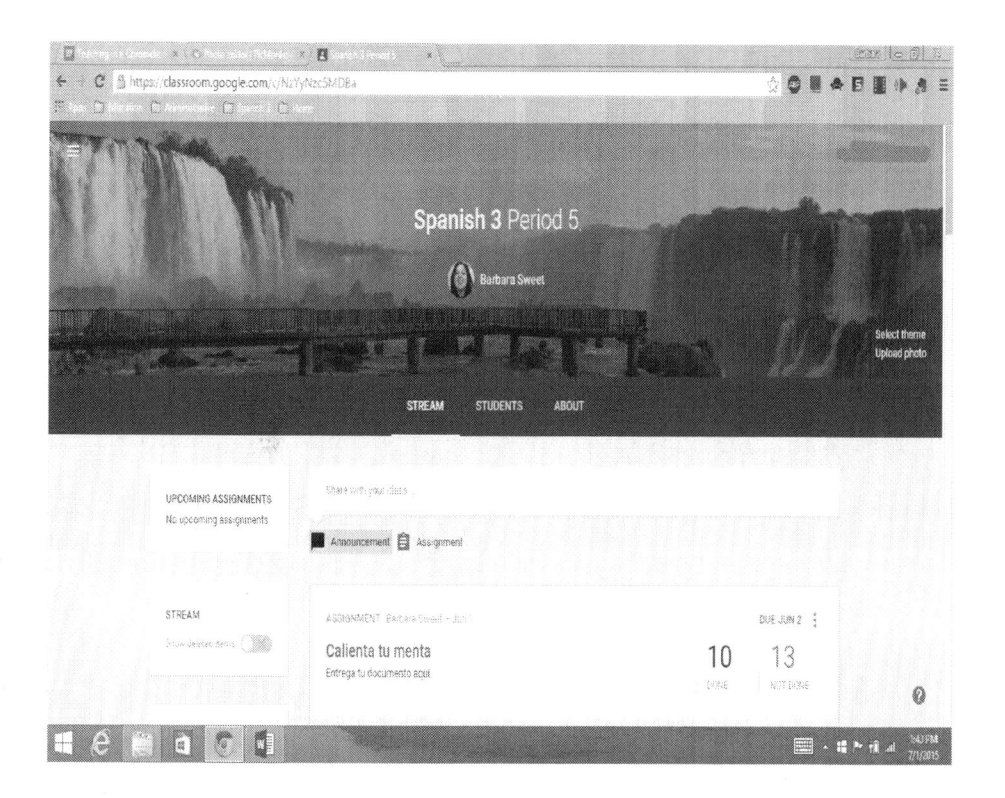

Other Google products I use a lot are: **Google Voice, Google Forms, and Google Drawings. Google Voice** allows you to set-up a local phone number and voice message. Some teachers use this as a way of having students be able to leave them voice messages after hours, without giving out their personal phone numbers. I don't use it that way. I use it as an oral assessment. Students are given a question, usually an open-ended question. They have a deadline like they would any other assignment. Students call the number. First they say their name and class period. This helps me keep track of who the message is from. Then, they have 2 minutes to provide their answer to the question. All the recordings are saved on the cloud and are downloadable to mp3. There was one time when I couldn't hear the name of the student in the recording. However, from Google Voice I was able to text the student and ask him for his name and I was able to give him credit for the work. Students who argue that they got a zero on the assignment, but really did call, can easily be verified. Simply type the phone number in the search box and it will show you all calls placed from that number. I teach a foreign language, but it can be used in other subjects. Have students call and explain a concept that you went over in class today. Have them state an opinion on a topic, etc.

When I grade Google Voice assignments, I sit down in front of the computer with Google Voice on one screen and my gradebook in another. I listen to the recordings one by one. I don't use a formal rubric, but I guess informally, I do. I grade them based on comprehension, did they include what I was looking for in the response, and was it submitted on time. I usually encourage students to write out their response and to practice saying it aloud a few times, then placing the call.

Google Forms allows you to create forms or surveys. You can use them to assess your class, like in a short quiz or test, or you can use them to gather information.

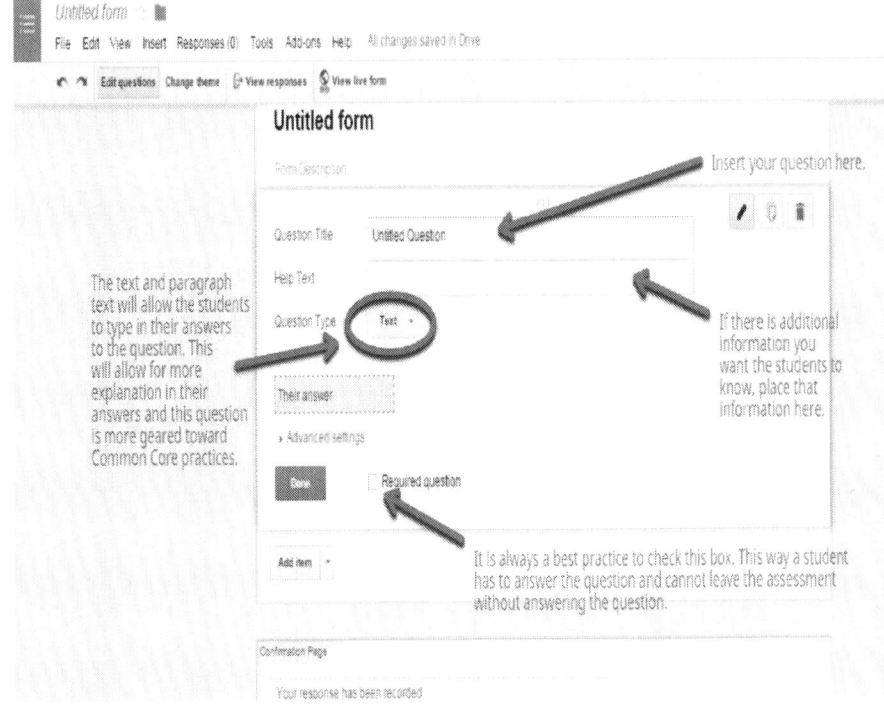

I've seen teachers use Google Forms in a variety of ways, including making short interactive stories where students are taken to a different page depending on the choices they make. Google Forms allows you to change the theme of the form, making it look more appealing. You can pick from a variety of question types, like fill-in, multiple choice, paragraph response, etc. I use Google Forms for short assessments and when I want to poll students. Instead of saying raise your hand if … -it's easier to use Google Forms and readily keep track of the overall responses. I teach 168 kids a day, so keeping track of the overall responses would otherwise be hard.

Google Drawings allow you to create images and download them as png or jpg files. It's a simple drawing program and not complicated or expensive like Adobe Photoshop. In my class I have students create Google Drawings as way to gauge comprehension. For example, if we are discussing Cinco de Mayo, I will ask students to create a drawing that includes something they learned. Google Docs and Google Draw are connected. You can use Google Draw separately, but if students are already typing in a Google Doc, then you can click on Insert and pick Drawing, which will open a Google Draw window. Once you are done with the drawing, it will insert it into your document.

4 EXTENSIONS, ADD-ONS, & APPS

Understanding the difference between extensions, add-ons, and apps was very confusing as it all sounded like the same thing to me. The more I've played with all of them, the more sense it has made. Here's my explanation in simple terms, hope it helps. The only browser you can have on a Chromebook is Chrome. An extension extends the capabilities of the browser. It allows it to do more than it normally would. An add-on works within one program. For example, an add-on in Google Sheet can allow you to auto-grade assessments. This add-on does not work within other programs, only Google Sheet. An app is a shortcut to something that is online.

Where do you find all this? All of these can be found in the Google Chrome Web Store. To find the Web Store on a Chromebook, click on the magnifying class on the bottom of the screen, and then on the icon for the Web Store (shown below).

Web Store

Magnifying glass  then .

You can also add add-ons from within the program. For example, Google Docs has an add-ons tab on the top of the screen. If you click on it, it will give you the option to get add-ons. You can then search for the one you are looking for. You only have to add add-ons once, after that you can find them by clicking add-on on the top of the page and picking the one you want to use.

The beauty of extensions, add-ons, and apps is that it's free. Google does not allow companies to add their service unless you can use it for free. Some companies do have premium services, but you can usually work without needing to pay for the premium. Programs that would normally require you to download software onto your pc are on the Chromebook, transformed into an extension or add-on. For example, my husband uses the program Gimp, which is an art editor program. In order to use it online, you need to download software onto your device. If you look for Gimp in the Chrome Web Store, you will find that it's an extension.

There are literally hundreds, even thousands of different extensions, add-ons, and apps. How do you choose? I would recommend starting with a few basic ones. Become familiar with those and comfortable using them. As your comfort level increases, you will be more willing to try newer ones. I caution you to not install hundreds of extensions and add-ons all at once. They will crowd your toolbar and even overwhelm you. You also want to think about your subject area. What do you need to be able to do in order to teach your subject? For example, the Chemistry teacher at my school wanted to be able to write chemical equations. I suggested MolView. It allows the student to create the chemical equation and view the molecule in either 2D or 3D.

Here are some suggestions of some basic ones to get you started.

Category	Name	Brief Description
Mindmapping	Mindmeister	Create mind maps of concepts.
Mindmapping	Coggle	Create mind maps of concepts. Automatically saves to Drive.
Assessment	PollEverywhere	Quickly create a poll to check for understanding.
Assessment	ProProfs QuizMaker	Create online quizzes and tests.
Assessment	Socrative	Fun game-like quizzes.
Grading	Flubaroo	Auto-grades quizzes in Google Sheets.

Screenshots	Awesome Screenshot	Take a picture of the screen and annotate on it.
Organization	myHomework	Digital agenda. Set it up to give reminders and give priority to certain classes.
Reading	Speak It	Highlight words and it reads them for you. Good for ELL students.
Reading	Evernote Clearly	Clears the webpage and makes it less distracting to read.
Productivity	Easy Accents	Allows you to choose accents for a variety of languages.
Productivity	Doc to Form	Upload your old

		worksheets as docs, turn them into a Google Form.
Productivity	g(Math)	Write Math problems in Docs.

Are you still using scantrons to grade quizzes and tests? There is a faster way to grade. Start by installing the extension Flubaroo to your Google Sheets. Go to this link https://goo.gl/DralHr. It is case sensitive, so make sure to put in the capital letters.

Now create a quiz using Google Forms. I suggest you add a question in your Google Form for the students to put their name. If you teach multiple periods of the same course, include another one for the students to include the class period. This will make grading easier later on.

Next, have the students complete the quiz. If you stand in the back of the room, and you have all students facing forward, you will be able to see all screens at once. I tell students that they can only have one tab open and any additional tabs is an automatic zero, no questions asked. You will also need to complete the quiz, since it will be used as the key that Flubaroo will use.

Google Forms will automatically create a Google Sheet with the students' responses. Go to the Google Sheet by clicking on the View Responses tab on the top of the Google Form.

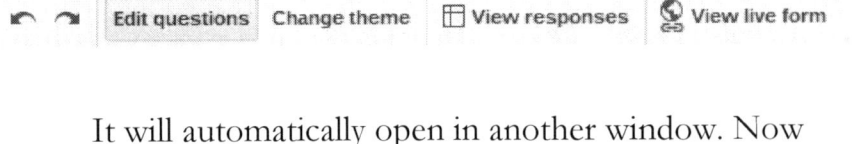

It will automatically open in another window. Now you will have to enable Flubaroo to run on the Google Sheet. Click on Add-ons, Flubaroo, and then Enable Grading.

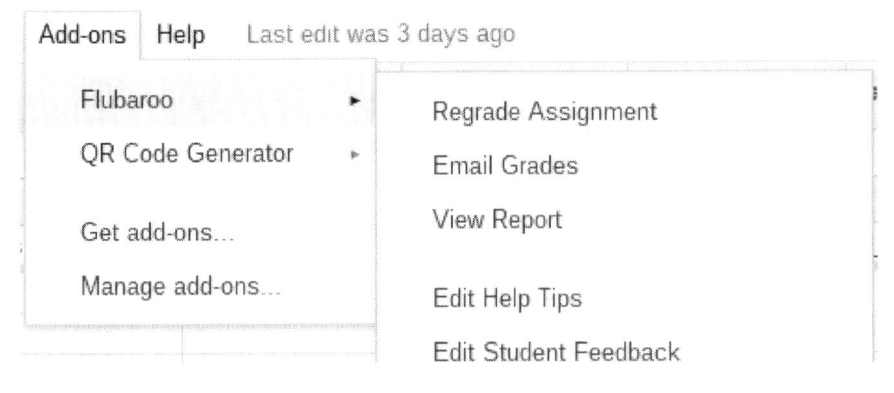

Mine says regrade assignment because I have already graded it. You can regrade assignment/quiz when a student is absent and has to take the quiz at another time. Next Flubaroo will guide you to grading the assignment. You will need to pick the grading option for each of the questions.

Grading Option

Normal Grading

Identifies Student
Skip Grading
Normal Grading
Grade by Hand (New!)

For example, the name question identifies the student, not normal grading. Next, pick your response from the list as the answer key. Press Continue. It will say grading completed once it's done. It only takes 1 or 2 minutes for Flubaroo to grade the assignment/assessment. Flubaroo will create another page in your Google Sheet called Grades. You will see it on the bottom.

Flubaroo highlights in red the students who performed poorly. It also marks in yellow the questions that several students got wrong. You can then reteach the material or curve the quiz by eliminating the question, etc.

5 HOW TO LEARN WITH A CHROMEBOOK

When my students first got their Chromebooks, they said, "We're not going to use our Chromebooks in your class, right?" I asked, "Why?" They said, "Because this is a Spanish class and these are for taking notes and writing essays, like in English class." I giggled to myself, realizing they didn't understand the power of technology in education. They assumed the Chromebook would only be used to type information and nothing more. This meant as I was teaching them how to use their Chromebook, I also needed to teach them how to learn with it. It was a new adventure. One they hadn't experienced before.

Our school provided the students with an initial training on how to carry and take care of their Chromebooks. We also gave them a procedure to follow when it wasn't working properly. The students knew they were responsible for the device and needed to care for it.

Our students quickly personalized their devices. They changed the screen saver. Found out how to change the background to the Chrome tabs, and even how to personalize their Gmail. At the beginning, this helped them feel like it was theirs. We understood and allowed it - as long as their personalization did not go against school policy.

Some students are easily distracted. Now that they had a cool new electronic device in front of them, their focus was on the technology and not the lesson's content. I have taken measures to ensure they were listening to me while I was explaining or teaching.

I use Class Dojo as my behavior management system.

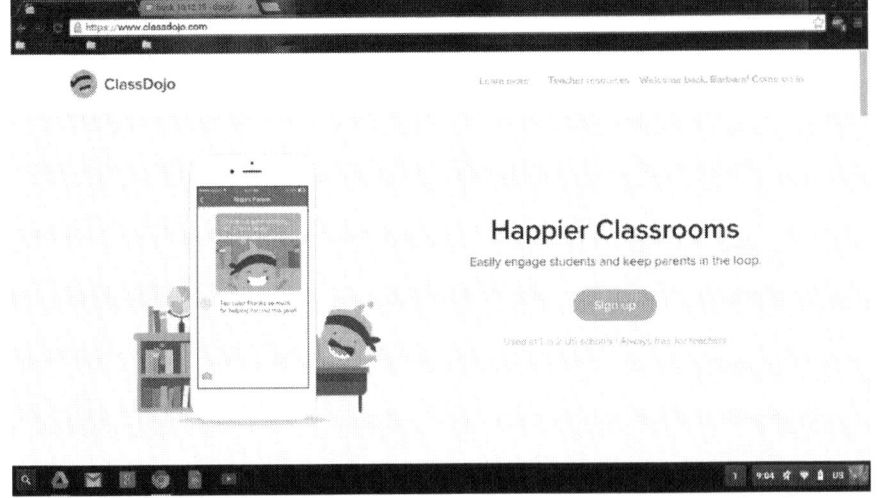

It's a free online program that allows you to give and take

away points depending on a student's behavior. In my class, Class Dojo is tied into their participation points and participation in my class counts for 40% of their grade. Students need to get 25 Dojo points per quarter. There is a free mobile app that students download and I code so I can give them and their parents access their progress. Since you can modify the behaviors in Class Dojo, I added inappropriate use of technology as one of my negative behaviors. I taught students that when I said to close their Chromebooks, I would wait until everyone did so before continuing on with my lesson or explanation. They were not allowed to open the lids until I said so and if they disobeyed me, they would get a negative point. Because my participation points are so heavily weighted, students work hard to get the points and it helps to deter negative or unwanted behaviors.

You want to create a culture for learning. I also made it clear that when I gave them instructions to do a task on their Chromebook, that's what I expected them to do. If I saw them opening other tabs and not following my instructions, they would also get negative points. Whatever behavior management system you choose, make sure that it includes the use of the Chromebooks. Clear expectations from day one is important in order to establish consistency in the classroom.

I use Remind to send students text or email reminders. It's a good way to remind students of upcoming tests, projects, and materials that they will need for class. It's easy to set-up and free. Go to remind.com, once you set it up, it will give you a code that you will give the students. Students then follow the instructions and send a text to that number. Students who don't have a phone can receive the reminder via email. You send the messages through the website, which keeps you from having to share your personal phone number with students. I caution you to not over use it. Students don't want to get six text messages a day for your class. Keep in mind that if another teacher is also using Remind, your text is not the only one he/she is receiving.

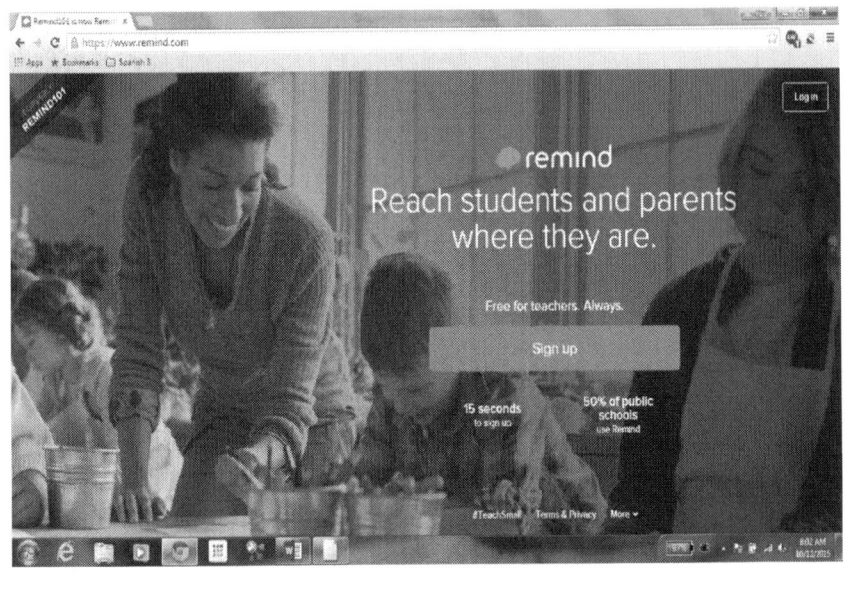

After explaining all of this and training my students to follow my instructions, I made a mistake that I will share with you so you don't make the same one. I was trying to go over a homework assignment that was in their textbooks. I noticed that some of my students were distracted looking at their screens. I told them all to close their Chromebooks and so they did. The next day before class, one of my students came up to me and said, "Are we going to be able to use our digital textbook, you told us yesterday to close our

Chromebooks." That was good feedback for me. Looking at the screen didn't automatically mean they weren't doing something related to my class. This year I plan to move my desk to the back of the room where I can more closely keep an eye on their screen activities.

As the months went by, students were being challenged to apply what they were learning in my class and demonstrated their knowledge with the use of a variety of technology tools. One of my students said, "This is hard. Can't you just go up there and talk for an hour?" I smiled. I realized that students had been conditioned to being passive in their learning. All they had to do was sit in the class quietly and pretend they were listening to the teacher. With Chromebooks in the classroom, they now had to apply, create, and construct their own knowledge. For the lazy students, it meant more work. It also meant a deeper understanding of the subject and mostly, an even more fun way to learn.

My students needed to learn how to read text online. I believe it's a necessary 21st century skill. My students complained about how they would rather write down their work on paper and how they preferred to read from a printed book. I did my best to explain to them that I truly believed that they were learning skills that were necessary for their future.

I, too, had a hard time transitioning from a paper book to an ebook. I was one of those people who would get a document emailed and print it out before I would read it. The reality was that reading printed text is what I was used to; it was what I was comfortable with. I slowly pushed myself to read more and more text on a computer, and now it's not a big deal. In fact, I like reading on my e-reader because all my books come with me anywhere I go. Since I like to travel, I often struggled with finishing my book and not wanting to carry a replacement book or not finding another book I liked as much. Of course that also meant taking into consideration the weight and thickness of the books. E-readers have come a long way. Now they are designed to look like the pages of the book so that the reader has more of a true paper reading experience.

I'd like to see more ebooks being used in classrooms. I know a French teacher, who with grant money, purchased 10 or 12 Kindle e-readers. She loads them with a variety of French novels and students check them out with her. They read their novels and then return the device to the teacher. She expressed how difficult it is to find "good" printed novels in French. It was much easier to buy digital versions and she would ultimately spend less money on them.

How can you use ebooks on a Chromebook? Easy. Students can install the Kindle app. You can create a school account and purchase books from there. If you are an English or Social Studies teacher, there are websites where you can read books for free that are no longer in copyright. My Spanish students are required to bring a silent reading book to class every day. I give them the option of doing a paper or digital text. Many of them have decided to use the digital version because it's easier to change books and they don't have to carry something extra to class every day.

Google Play Edu allows you to push out books to not only Android tablets, but also Chromebooks.

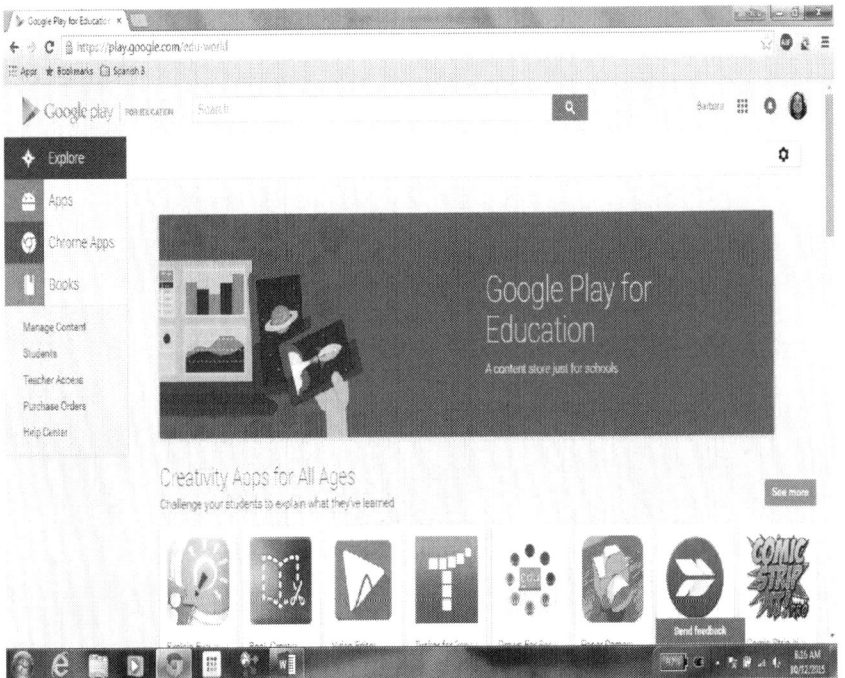

However, I haven't found this to be a good solution for our school. The cost is per user on the book and you only get a limited amount of reuses and as such, it becomes too costly. However, it does have a lot of the free copyright (public domain) texts. At my school, I'm the only one with authority to push Google Play apps and books out to the teachers and students. You might have to ask your IT department to see who handles that.

Sometimes you will want students to read a particular webpage. Maybe you want them to analyze it, find the main points, think of the author's point of view, etc. One way to clear the webpage of unnecessary ads and often distracting information, is to use an add-on called Clearly. It will clear the page and only shows you the text. You can then use an add-on called Texthelp Study Skills: Highlighting Tools. This tool gives you 4 different color highlighters: yellow, blue, green, and pink. You can then tell the student to highlight specific information in a specific color. For example, highlight the main idea yellow and the conclusion green. At the end, this add-on allows you to gather the information by color. The teacher can then project the answer document and discuss what the students put together.

Years ago, I took a workshop called Step up to Writing. The presenters showed us a technique where the students had to highlight the printed text with 3 colors: pink, yellow, and green. I think each color represented part of a sandwich: the bread, the meat, and the toppings. The problem was when the student erroneously highlighted a section of the text the wrong color, there was no good way of changing it. This becomes a non-issue with this great add-on.

6 LESSON PLANNING

It takes time for students to learn a new program. Plan time to explain it. Connect your computer or Chromebook to the projector or SMARTboard and have them follow you as you explain how to use the new tool. Give the students time to play with the new tool. Students like exploring and trying to learn how to do more than what you thought it could do. Let them teach you.

After I've explained how to use the program, I write some step-by-step simple instructions on the board. That helps my special needs students follow at their own pace and remember the steps. It also keeps me from repeating myself 20 times. I just point to the board. If you are using Google Classroom, you can give the steps to the students as an announcement.

You know how they use to say "plan for a rainy day?" In the world of technology, you want to plan for a day without Wi-Fi. How are you going to conduct your lesson if you suddenly don't have Internet? Always have a plan B.

Be flexible. I will often give students a specific set of instructions. For example, I want you to work with your partner and create a Google Doc that contains a response to the questions, an image, and your opinion. However, students will often want to add something or demonstrate their understanding of the material some other way - allow them the flexibility to do so.

Start with your subject area in mind. What concepts do your students need to learn in chapter 1? Pull those concepts out. Think of ways to use technology to enhance their learning experience and understanding of those concepts. For example, you're covering a unit on habitats. Instead of having the students cut out pictures of animals and habitats and glue them on paper, have them create an online product. Link videos and resources that relate to their topic. Have them explore what the problems currently are related to that habitat and have them find ways to solve them. Allow the students a chance to share their work with one another and the world. Have students create an e-portfolio, blog, or web page. Have them keep the artifacts of learning they are creating and put them all in one place.

Think of the age level and skill set of your students. Is the technology you plan to implement too easy or too hard for them? Maybe you want to just experiment and see. I've taught every grade level PK-12. Sometimes I don't know if a tech tool will work or not. Sometimes I think they will love it and it turns out to be too easy or the other way around. I make a mental note of what worked and what didn't so that the next time I teach that age group I don't make the same mistake.

Tech time and other time. I use technology a lot in my class, but that doesn't mean that students can't use other tools. I still do a lot of hands-on activities and games. It's also not good to have students staring at a computer screen all day. Plan a break in between where students can get up and move around. I like doing a gallery walk activity once in a while. That's where I post a series of images and or questions around the room. I divide the students into small groups.

Students rotate around the room at the sound of a chime and either discuss the image or answer the questions orally. It keeps the students engaged in my subject area, practicing vocabulary, and gives them an opportunity to stretch their legs and talk.

Use the SAMR Model. I've included an image of the SAMR Model which was developed by Dr. Ruben R. Puentedura. Please take a moment to look at it. His work titled, *SAMR Approaches to Implementation*, provides examples of the implementation of technology in education at various stages. The acronym SAMR represents: Substitution, Augmentation, Modification, and Redefinition. At the substitution stage, the teacher is simply changing something from the lesson by substituting it with technology. An example of this is instead of writing an essay on paper, the student types it in Google Docs. In augmentation, the teacher is still substituting something in the lesson with the use of technology, but now something else is learned because of the technology. Modification allows for a significant change in the lesson. In redefinition, the student is able to do more than was ever possible before because of the use of technology. As you are planning your lessons, keep this model in mind. Which letter is your lesson in the SAMR Model? Once you've taught the lesson, reflect on what you can do to move up a stage the next time you teach it.

Substitution	Technology is a direct substitute with no functional change.	Use Google Earth instead of an Atlas to locate a place.
Augmentation	Technology is a direct substitute with some improvement to function.	Use Google Earth rulers to measure the distance between two places.
Modification	Technology permits you to significantly	Use Google Earth layers and 360 views to research

	redesign the lesson.	specific locations.
Redefinition	Technology allows the creation of tasks that weren't possible before.	Create a narrated Google Earth tour and share it with others online.

Include technology in your behavior management plan. You want to be able to control what students are doing on their Chromebooks and when. Walking around has always been my best strategy for keeping track of what students are doing on their computers. Implement a screen down and a consequence for not following your instructions. Tell students what websites they are allowed and not allowed to use during your class. Maybe you're okay with them playing games, if they have finished they work; maybe you don't want them to play games in your class at all.

What if a student works on other class work after they are done with your class work, is that okay with you? I find it interesting to see what my students are doing in other classes. Sometimes they are working on a project idea or website that I had never heard before. With technology constantly changing and updating, it's good to keep an open mind and willingness to learn new things. In my class, my students need to finish my work first. If they are done and waiting for their classmates to continue on with the lesson, then they are allowed to work on their other classes, but once we move on, they need to be willing to put that away and refocus on my subject. Establish clear expectations and this won't be a problem.

Close all tabs. I've found it useful to tell students to close all tabs except for the ones we are working on. Students are really fast and sneaky at switching between screens. They can have a game open in one tab and your work in another.

When you come by, they will switch from the game to the screen with the work, so that it looks like they were busy working all along. Students will also share a blank Google Doc with their friends and leave it open. When you walk away they use it as a means of chatting with their friends who are in a different class.

Furniture placement. I hate when I walk into a classroom and see long rows of desks - that tells me the teacher is still teaching the "old-fashioned way." Modern classrooms are very open. Furniture is movable and re-arrangeable according to the lesson and preferences of the learners. At the very least, students should be easily able to transition from working individually to working collaboratively. You should have procedures in place for this as well. Usually your furniture selection is limited to what the school has available, at which case you need to make the best out of what you've got. My desk is limited to where it is, because of the telephone jack and power outlet. I often disconnect my Chromebook and sit amongst my students. In addition to helping me better monitor what they are doing, it also helps me to build rapport with them. I'm not the authority who is always in front and in command, but I am approachable. If you have the option on putting your desk in a place where you can easily see all the computer screens of the students at one glance, then that would be ideal.

21st century skills. Realistically, by the time this year's Kindergarten students graduate from high school, new careers will exist. So our challenge as educators is to prepare our students today for the jobs of tomorrow. But, how do we do that if we don't know what they need to know or be able to do? We know that technology is something that isn't going away. It's not a fad. Technology is going to continue to grow and evolve. I think that learning how to type (with all fingers, not just one), reading on a screen, discerning between good sources of information online, online etiquette, etc., are all important things for students to learn. We also know that we need to develop critical thinking skills in our students. I've heard it be said, "if your students can Google the answer, you're asking the wrong questions."

While looking for information online, at times it is helpful to provide students with open-ended questions. This gives the students the opportunity to think beyond the norm and explore what might be possible. Which brings me to my next point, nurture creativity. We seem to allow students to be creative in elementary school and somehow we lose focus of that in later years and focus on assessments and grades. Let students create something that doesn't exist. Have them create a new app, a new invention, a new solution to a world problem. Make real-life connections with your subject area. Why focus on what your textbook says that was written 20 years ago? As you can imagine, I'm not a fan of following a textbook page by page. It's an archaic form of teaching – one, in my opinion, that definitely needs to change. We can't teach our students like we were taught.

Layers of understanding. Technology provides an opportunity for students to demonstrate their understanding in a variety of ways. Don't limit it to just one thing. Have the student create something, write about it, make a video about it, create a podcast or audio recording, etc. I call this layers of understanding. The repetition of concepts, but demonstrated in a different manner, helps ensure that the student first of all understands, but also that he/she is more likely to remember it later on.

Don't reinvent the wheel. There are plenty of good resources out there made by teachers for teachers. Google what you are trying to do and you will probably find some ideas on how to do it. YouTube and Teacherspayteachers are good places to find ideas and resources. Connect with other teachers on Twitter and Social Media. If you're not learning from Twitter, you're following the wrong people. Pinterest is also good place to get lesson ideas.

7 DIGITAL ARTIFACTS OF LEARNING

There are currently many tools available to help students create a product. As you know, the direction of education has shifted from being passive recipients of knowledge to active learners who create and find meaning to life's problems. I call a digital artifact anything a student creates with a digital tool that demonstrates their learning or makes their thinking visible.

Web 2.0 refers to websites that allow the user more than just static information. It allows you to create a digital product. Many of these digital artifacts can also be done with a Chrome add-on, extension, or app. However, sometimes you can do more with the web application then you can with the add-on, extension, or app.

Some digital tools include: audio recordings, collages, comic books, posters, slide presentations, digital books, and narrated slideshows, movies, animations, screencasts, and study guides.

Audio recordings can be used a variety of ways in a class. Students can create podcast type recordings narrating or explaining a concept. The teacher can use it to give audio feedback. This tool can be especially helpful for English language learners or students learning a second language. Students can listen to themselves and practice proper pronunciation. The teacher can leave an audio recording for the class with instructions. Another option is for the teacher to record herself asking questions and having students respond to her in their own audio recording.

Vocaroo is an online voice recording service. It's free and simple to use. Once you have completed your recording, simply click save. It will then give options as to how to share the recording. I usually use the web link. Students can insert the link into their work. It also gives you the option of sharing it directly on social media, downloading as an mp3 file, embedding, or emailing the recording. Like that's not awesome enough, on the bottom right, on top of the delete now button, it says QR code. If you click on that, it will give you the QR for your recording. You can have the kids talk about what they learned about their project, post the QR code with their work, and when parents come to Back-to-School night, they can see and hear what their child did in class.

Collages are a good way to gather various images about one person or theme in one place. Picmonkey, http://www.picmonkey.com/and Pixlr, https://pixlr.com/, give you image editing options and collage templates.

To make a collage:

Press collage on the top of the page.

A sub-menu will open asking you to pick where you will be uploading your photo from.

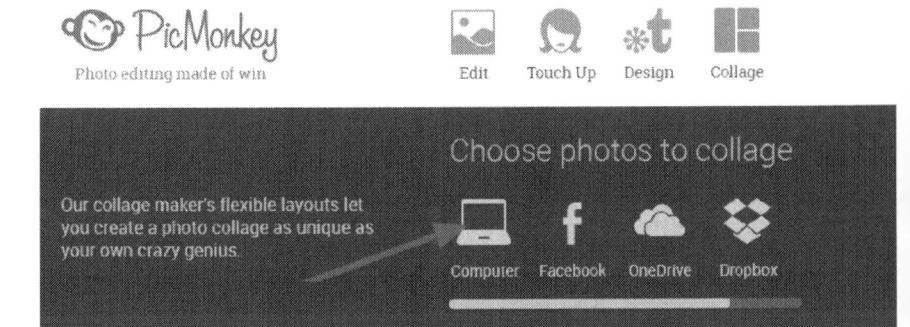

Click on open photos to continue to add more images to your collage. Add as many images as you need for your project.

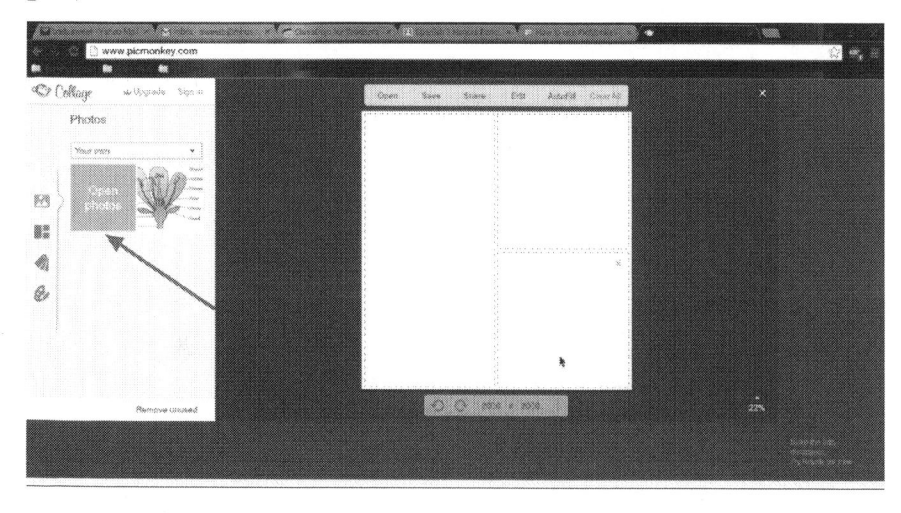

Now click and drag the image from the left to where you want it on the right.

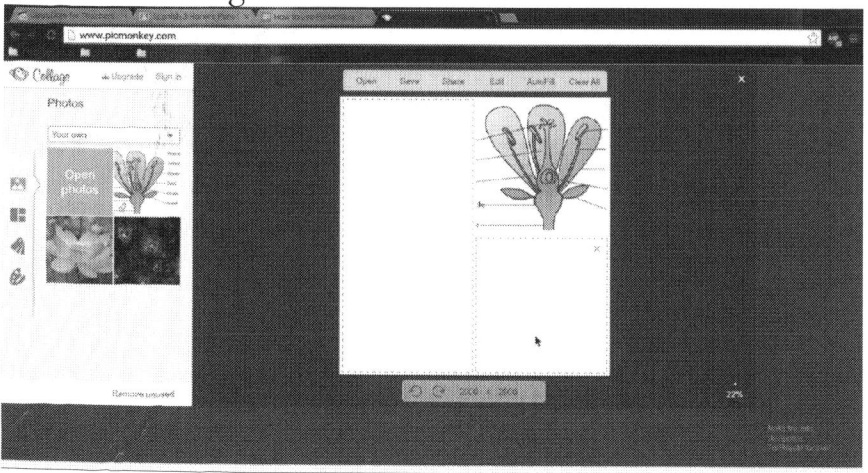

To change the template, click on the second icon on the left.

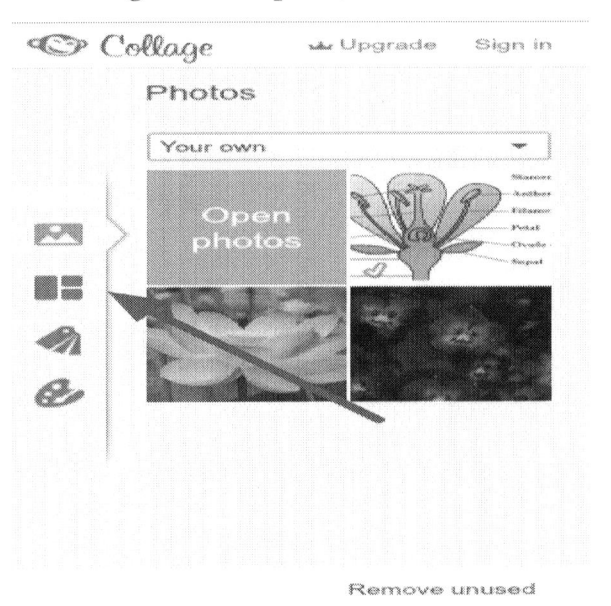

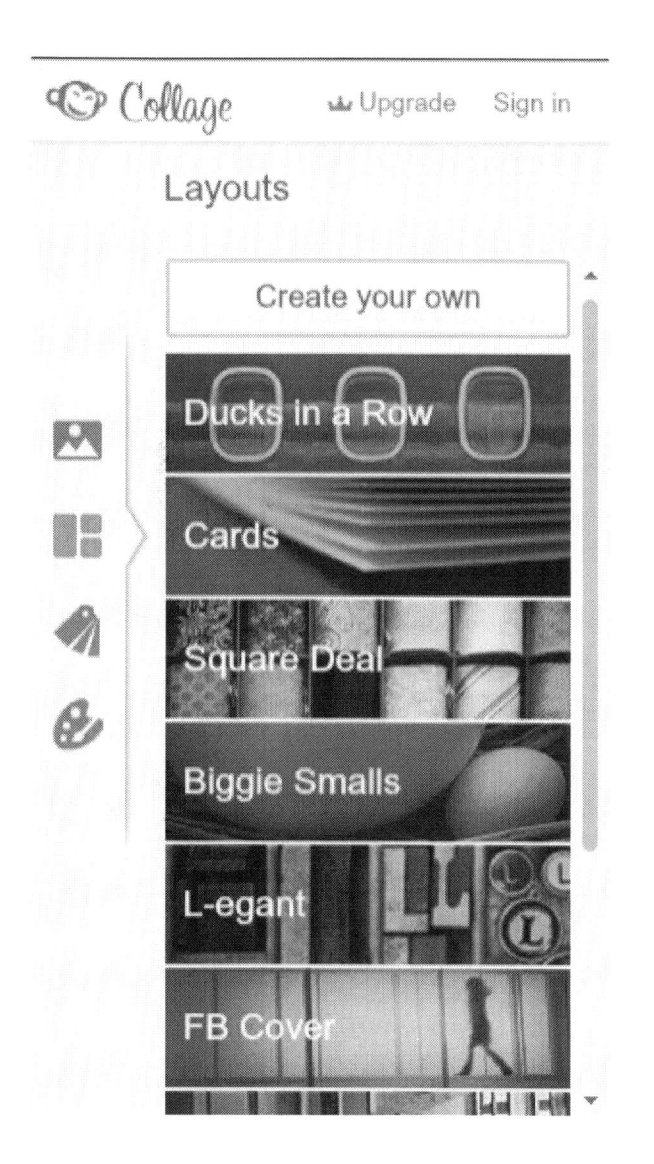

Click on the options on the right. It will open more sub-options for each category.

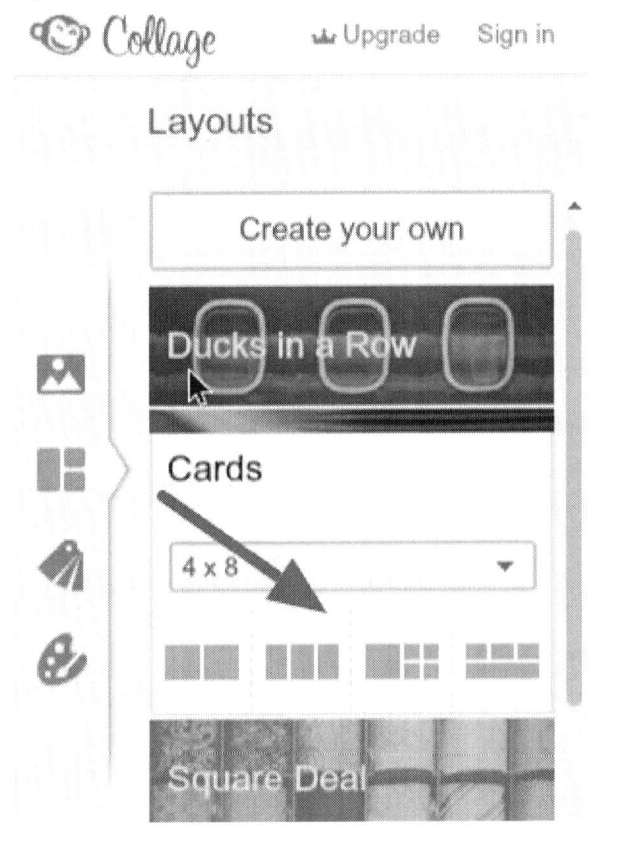

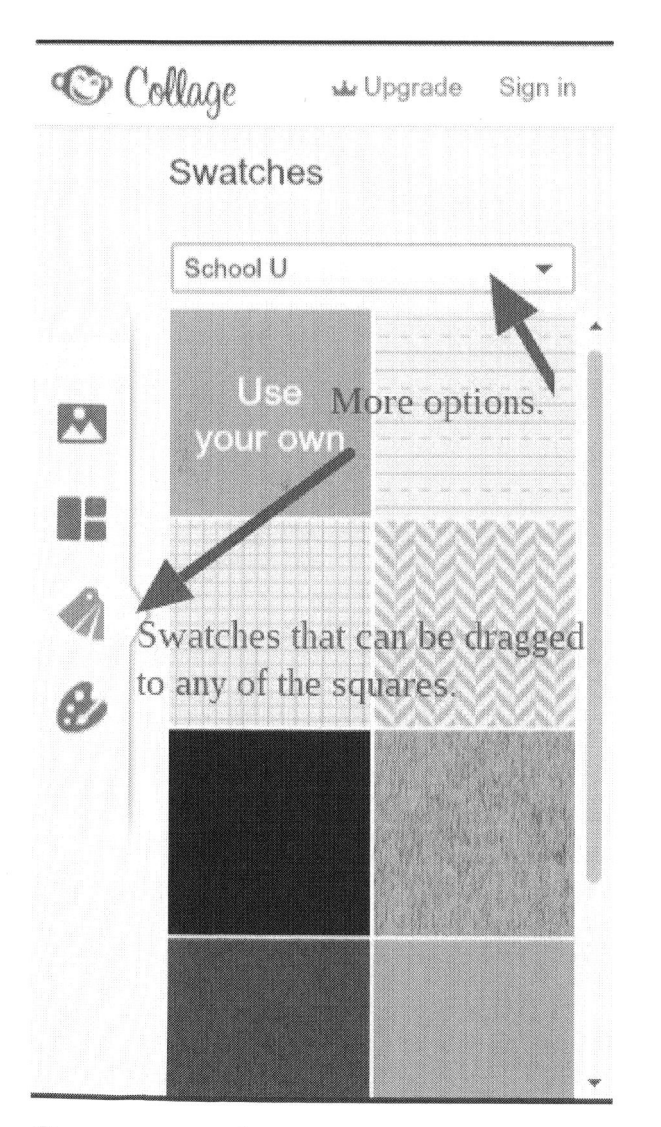

Once you are done arranging your photos, click on save.

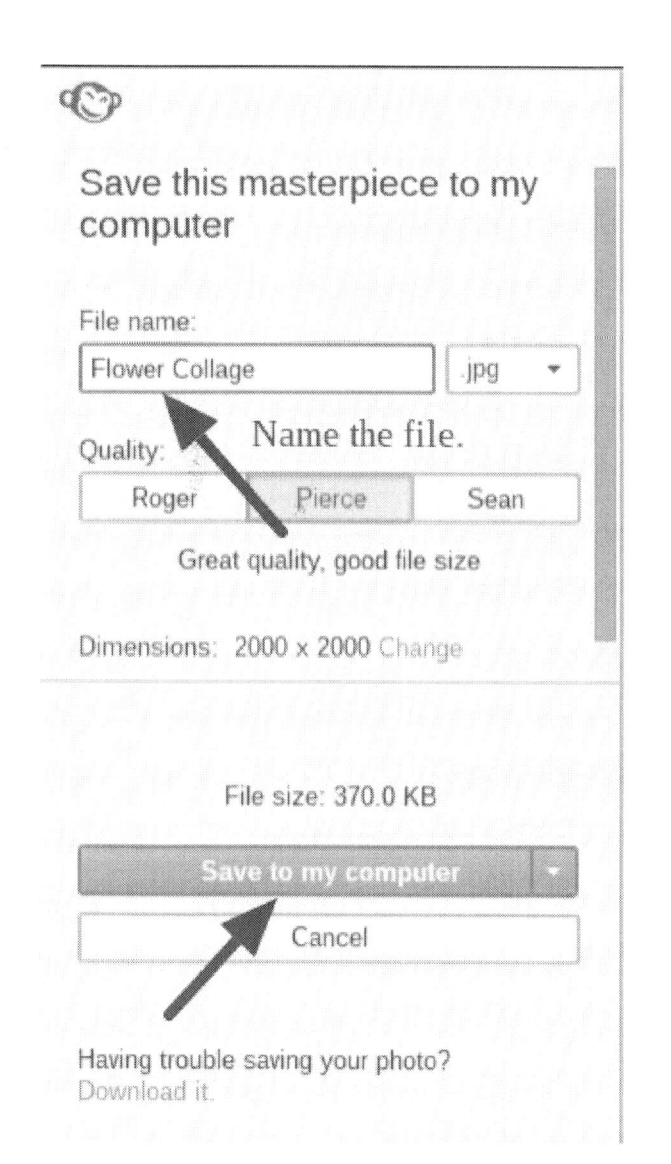

The following example provided gives you an idea of what is possible. Students learning about the life-cycle of the frog can gather images of the different stages and then put it together in a collage.

Screencasting has been my obsession for several years now. It was the topic of my doctoral dissertation research. While for my research I focused on undergraduate online students, the value of video and audio in learning remains the same. It provides the learner with a video recording that includes mouse movements, audio, video, and on-screen annotations. Screencasts are often referred to as screen captures or screen sharing. Those terms all mean the same thing.

YouTube has many videos that are screencasts. They typically are used on YouTube to show people how to do something. Khan Academy first started as a series of screencast videos that Salman Khan (founder) created to help his cousin with his math homework. The videos became so popular that he eventually quit his job and founded Khan Academy.

You can create screencasts using a Chromebook and some of the Chrome add-ons. Some of these include: Screencastify, TechSmith Snagit, and MediaCore Capture. You can also use Google Hangouts to create screencasts, but some schools block it.

What can you do with screencasting? Your imagination is the limit. Seriously. here are some possibilities:

1. You can create a flipped classroom. This is where students view a video at home and come into class

ready to do activities based on what they learned on the video.

2. You can pre-record your lesson showing Google Slides on the background, and a headshot of yourself explaining the content. Upload the link of the video to the students via Google Classroom and have them come into class ready to discuss the content.

3. My favorite and focus of my dissertation research was using screencasting to provide feedback to students. Imagine how powerful it would be to not only see written comments, but to hear your voice and seeing you go through their work.

4. Students can use it explain a concept. For example, studying the Civil War? Have students find an image of the Civil War that appeals to them. Have them upload it and create a screencast explaining the history behind the image. Isn't that more meaningful and fun than having you do a lecture on the same concept?

5. Have students create screencasts for other classes. For example, Spanish 3 students can create a video for Spanish 1 students. Calculus students can create a screencast helping their pre-calculus friends understand a math concept. Empower students by allowing them to teach others. We don't always have to be in the driver seat.

6. How about reading an online storybook to a first grade student and sending the link to the teacher to share?

7. How about using it for students to self-evaluate themselves or others? Have the students listen to their own videos and reflect on it.

Comic books. Comic strip stories allow the student to demonstrate understanding of a concept. It also makes it fun to create the character and develop their personalities. When I was in high school, my Chemistry teacher did many creative things in class, including having us create comic strips. We would cut one out of an old newspaper, cut out the speech bubble, and create a new one on paper. We would then glue the new speech bubble onto the comic strip. This was hard to do at times as we had to find old newspapers that had the character's position in a way that allowed for the conversation we wanted them to have to take place.

In my Spanish classes, I've had students draw it out. They fold a paper so that they have eight squares on one side of the sheet. Each square represents a box in the comic strip. Students then draw their characters, create the speech bubbles, and color it in. I've used this idea to have students practice a particular verb tense or a set of vocabulary words.

Now all of this can be done online. While there are many options, some of the ones I use are Pixton at pixton.com

and Make Belifs Comix at makebeliefsccomix.com.

Students can easily choose their characters, type in the speech bubbles, and share their work online.

Posters. Create a digital poster. You can use Canva available at canva.com

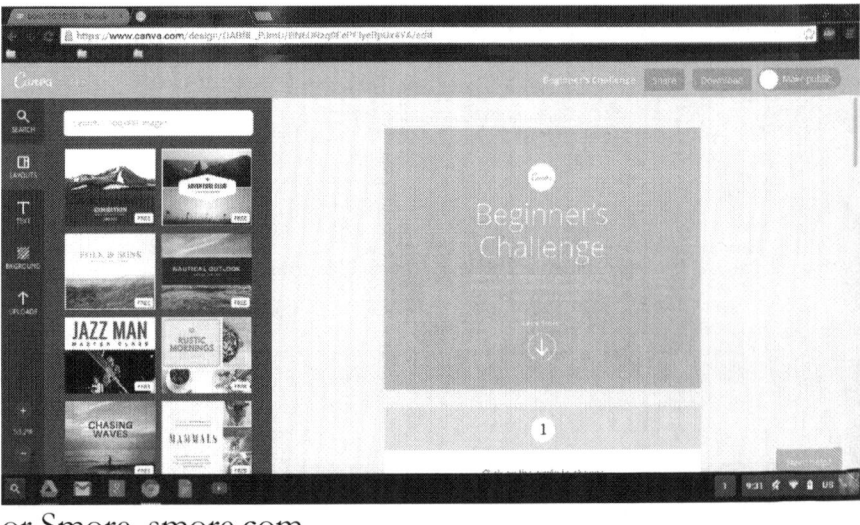

or Smore, smore.com.

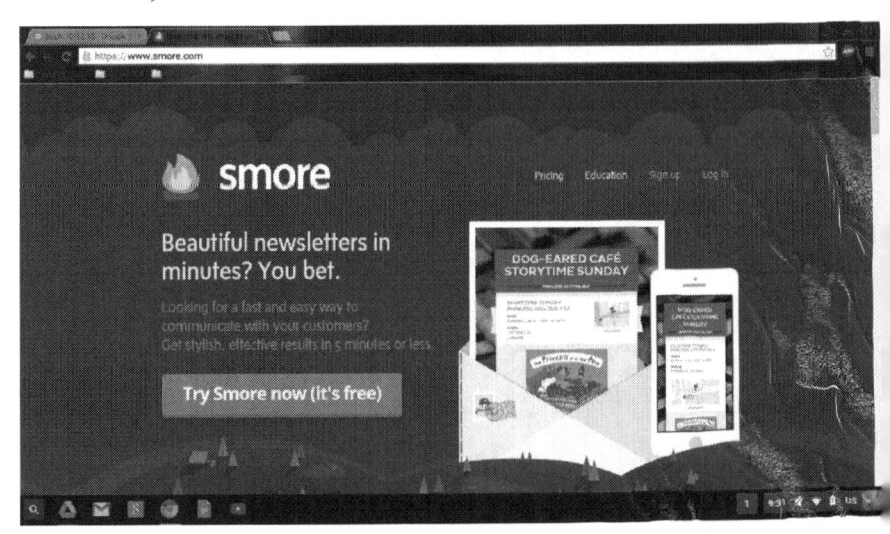

Remember that creative Chemistry teacher of mine, I also made a poster for her class with the elements. We had to choose one of the elements of the periodic table and create a poster that promoted the element. However, the element had to be advertised in a way that it would entice a person to buy it. It forced us to think of what the element could be used as and how to market it in a creative way. By the way, my teacher received a National Presidential Teaching Award and she got to meet the president. She has been an inspiration to me.

Create a Thinglink. A Thinglink is an image with which you can include a variety of links within it. For example, you can have a picture of a fruit basket and have links with it for each of the fruits. The individual links can take you to see a video or read more about the cultivation of that fruit, etc. It's a way of grouping a variety of sources into one place.

To create a Thinglink go to thinglink.com and create and account. Now select the create option on the top right of the screen.

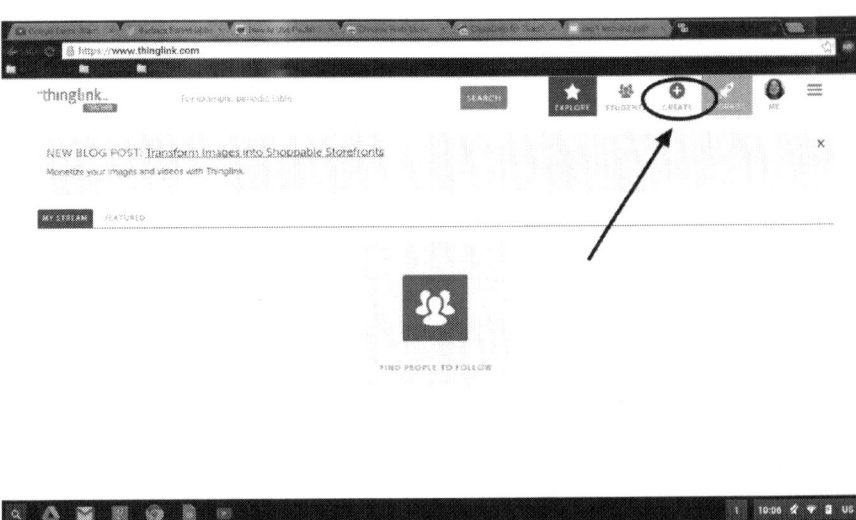

Choose the image that you want to upload.

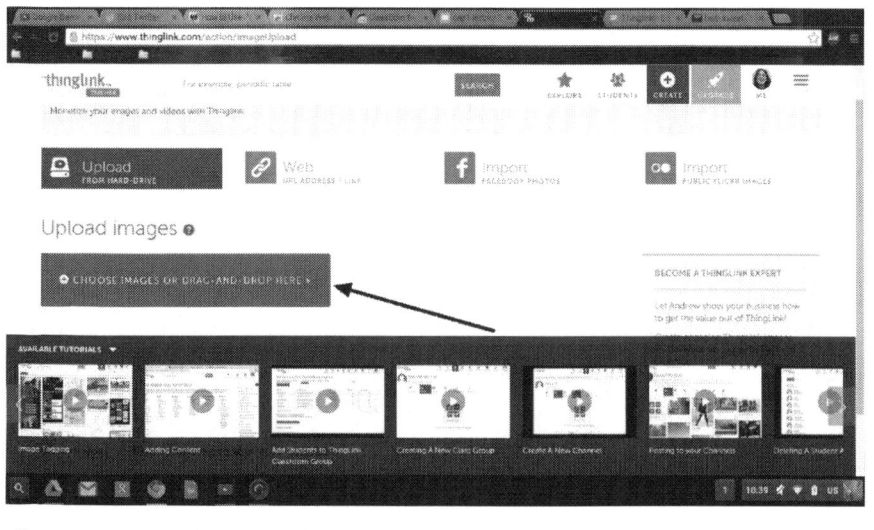

Once you've selected an image, give your Thinglink a title.

Click anywhere on the image to create a tag. It will look like a button.

It will automatically open a menu on the left of the screen. This is where you can put the web link to the source. It can be a video, image, doc, etc.

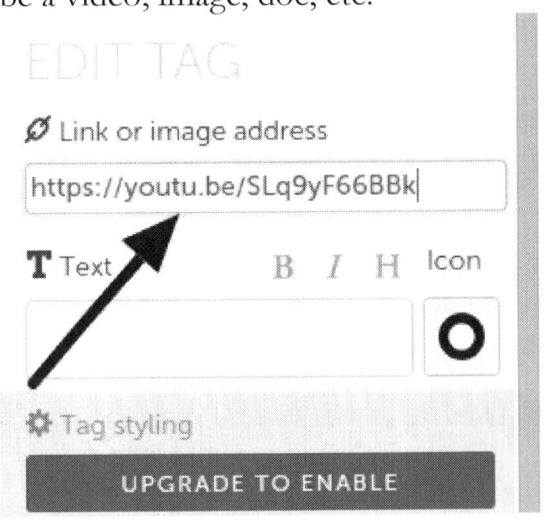

Clicking on the icon symbol will allow you to change the image. The free account only has access to some icons. If you want more, you will need purchase the premium version.

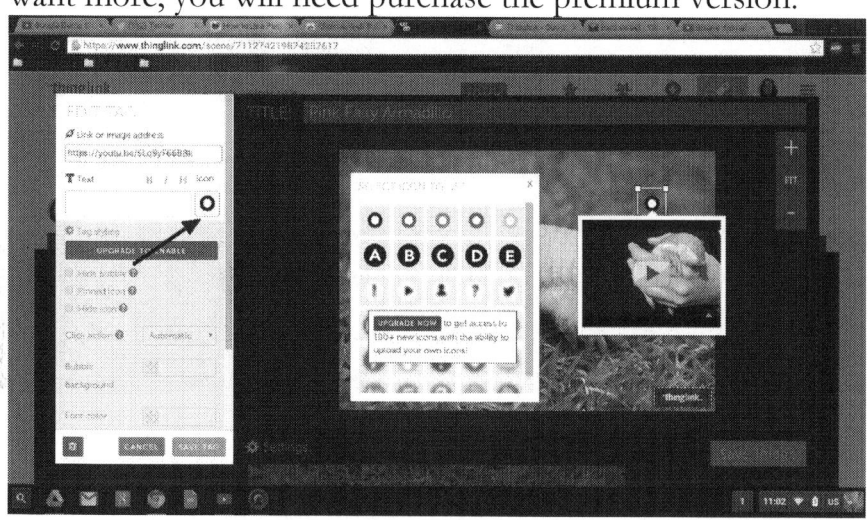

The icon will display on the right showing you a preview of what is being linked. You can write some additional text in the text box, if you wish. Then, press Save Tag.

Also, you can move the tag to anywhere on the image.

Find a variety of sources and add them as tags.

Click Save Image when you are done adding tags.

Now you can share your Thinglink. Press the share icon. A menu will pop up on the left with the url of your Thinglink.

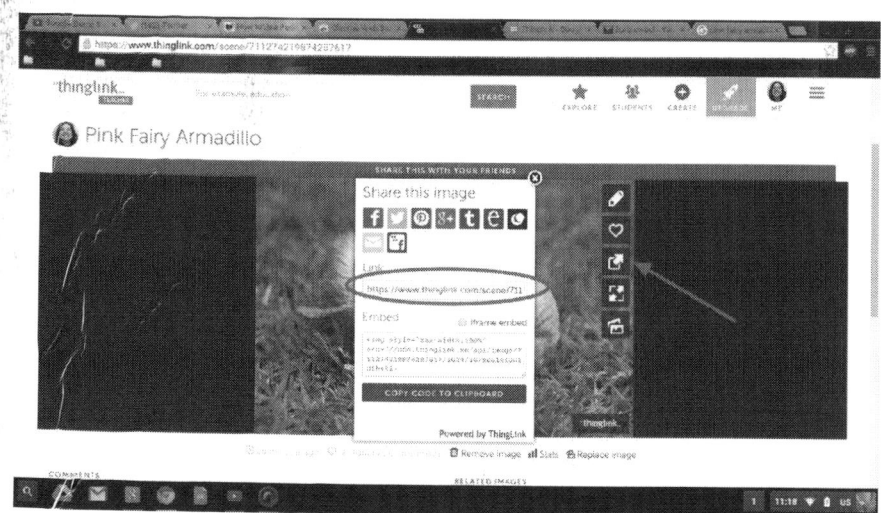

Here's an example of a Thinglink:

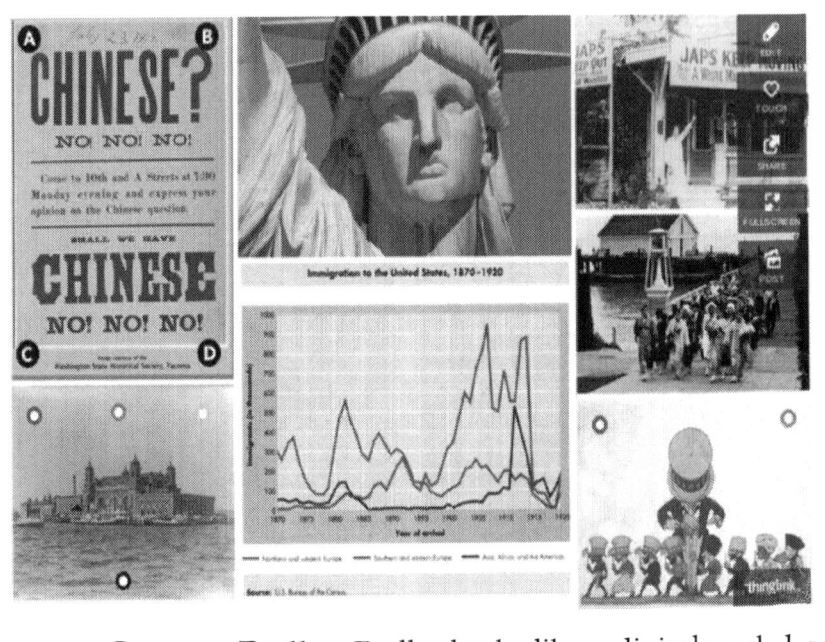

Create a Padlet. Padlet looks like a digital cork-board. You can choose from a variety of backgrounds. Students gather information on a topic and pin it to the Padlet. You can create one Padlet as a class and have everyone add to it or you can assign students to work on a particular topic as a group.

Go to padlet.com and create an account, then click on "create a new Padlet."

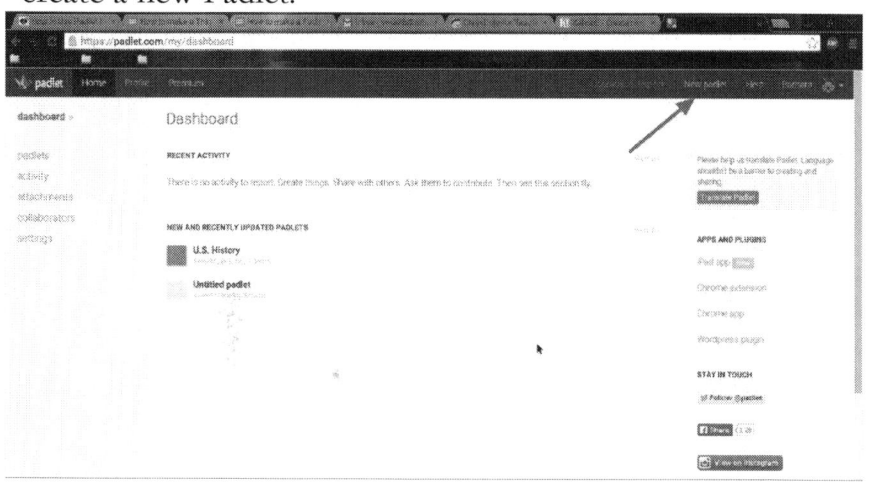

Click and drag images from your computer to the Padlet.

Click on the gear on the right to modify your Padlet.

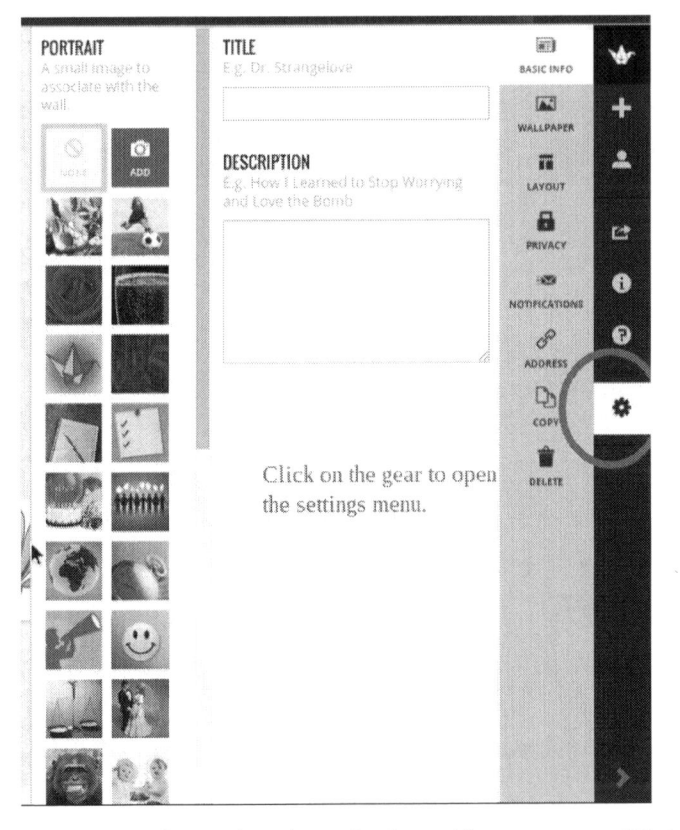

Enter a title and a description, if you want. Pick a portrait photo to have an image that will help you recognize your Padlet.

Select Wallpaper to change the wallpaper of your Padlet. There are many designs to choose from.

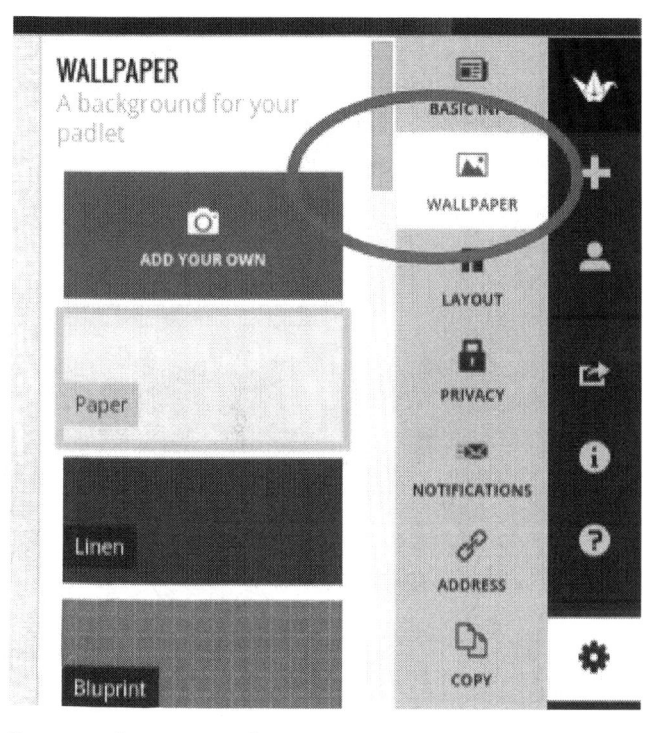

Layout lets you change how your images are displayed on Padlet.

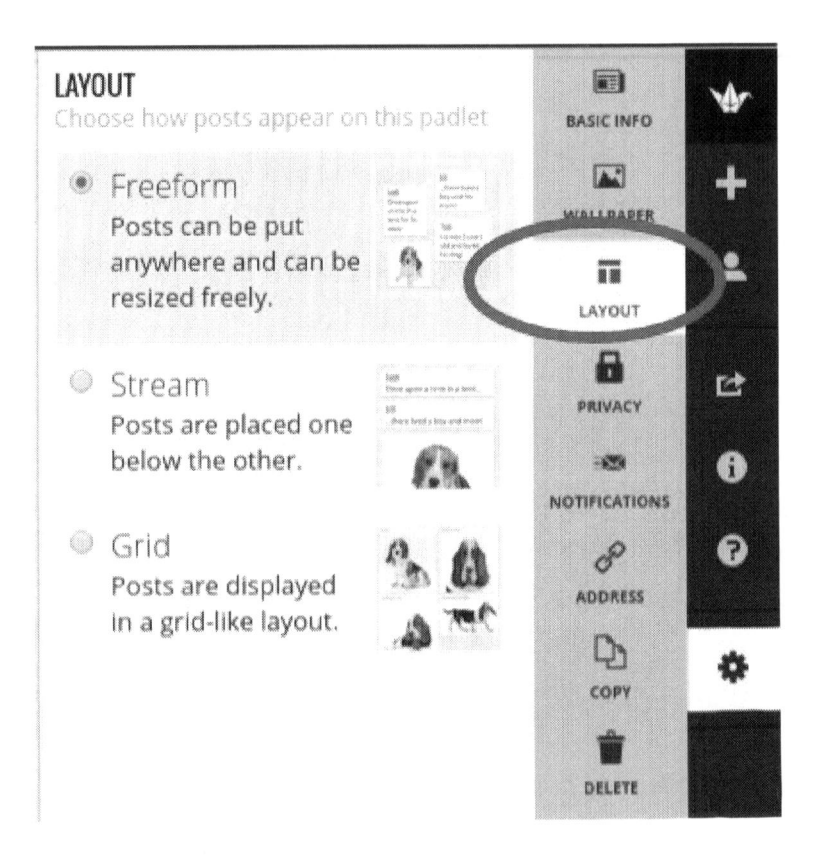

The privacy option lets you select whether you want to have your Padlet password protected, public, or private.

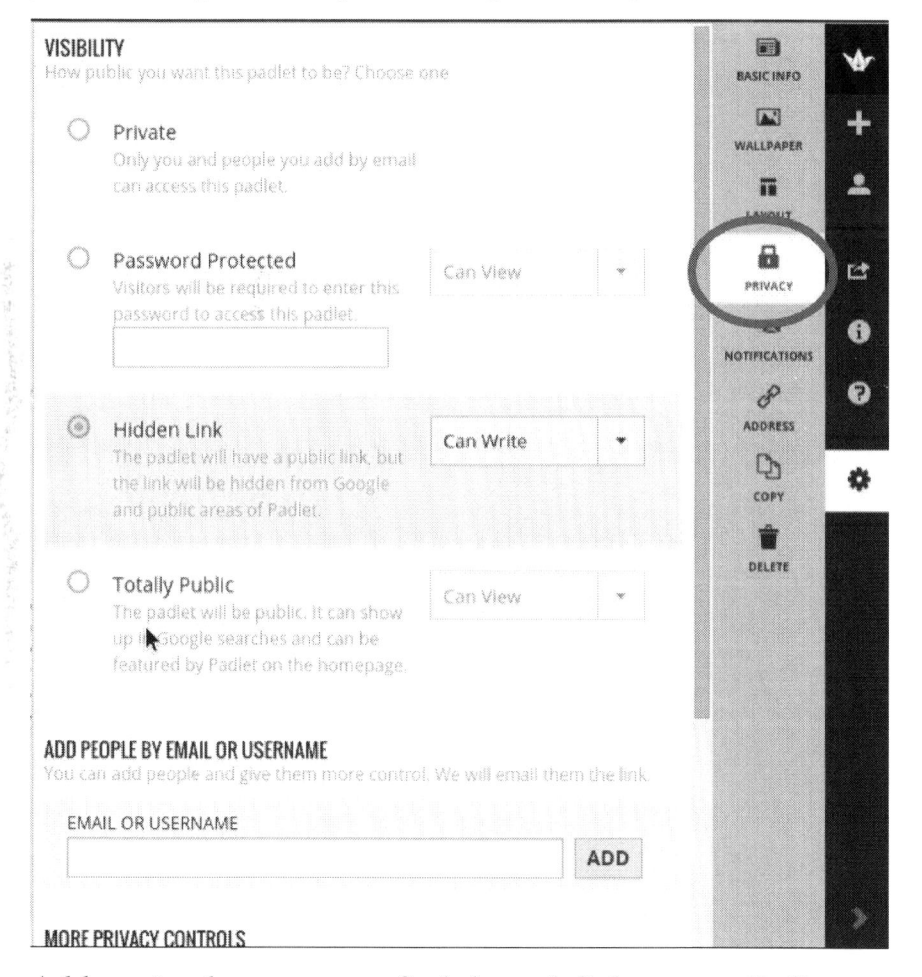

Address is where you can find the web link to your Padlet. You can also create your own custom url.

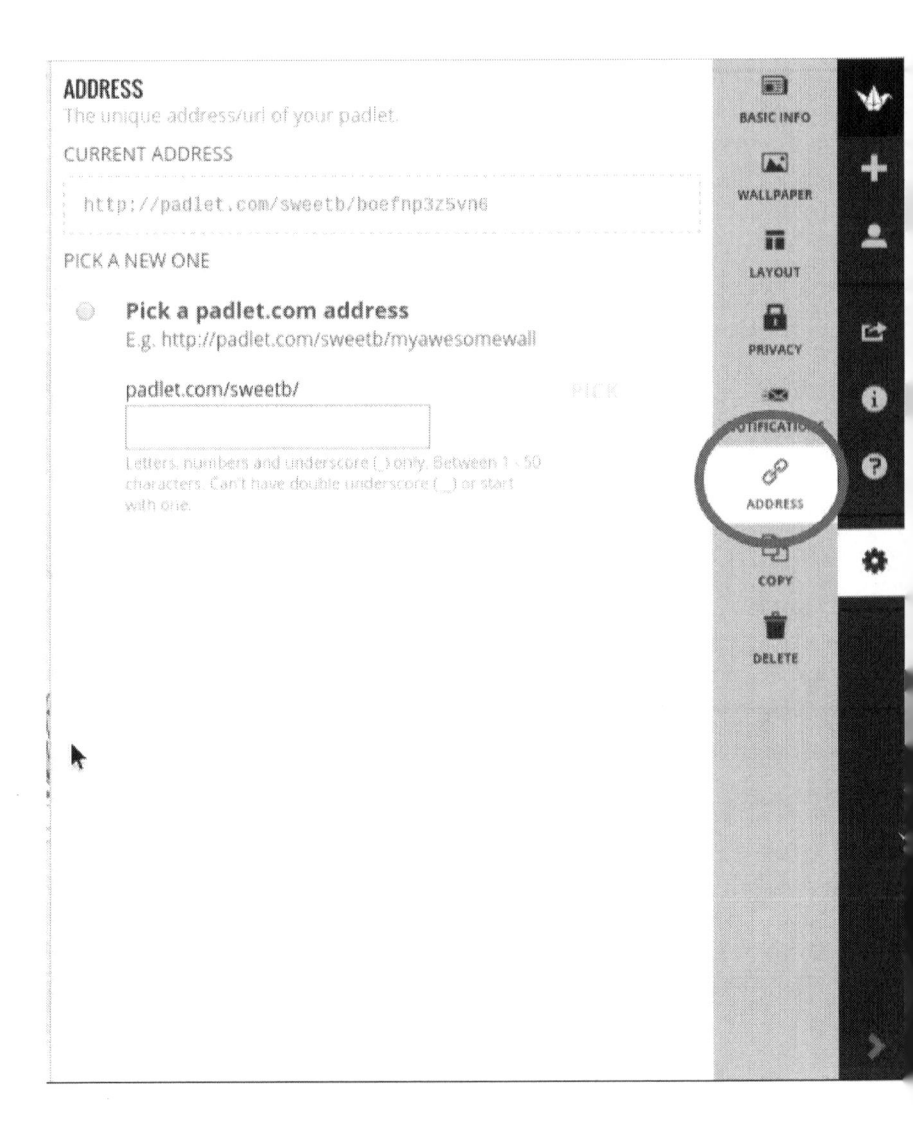

Slide presentations. You want a different way to present information, use Biteslide, biteslide.com.

Digital books. Want students to create their own digital books, use Simplebooklet, simplebooklet.com.

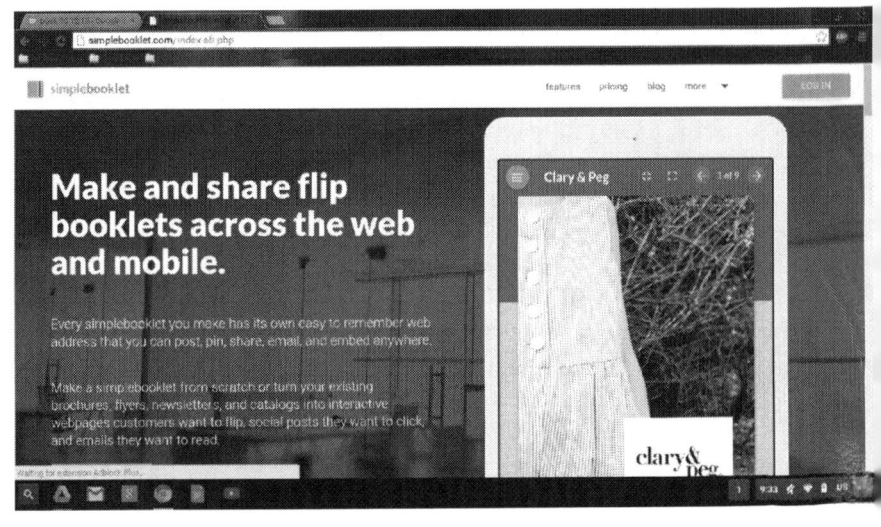

There are other sites, but the others tend to be more for creating yearbooks or photo albums. They also focus on trying to sell you the final product.

Narrated slideshows. I use to love using VoiceThread, but it is no longer free and priced ridiculously high. MoveNote allows you to record yourself narrating while going through a slideshow. It's an alternative to screencasting and a good presentational tool. Find it in the Chrome Web Store.

Movies. In addition to using YouTube, you can use WeVideo. My students love being able to create movies and show them to their classmates. The final project for my class is a video. Students are given three options of types of videos. They pick their groups and coordinate with them which option they want to do, how to do it, and where to film. I give them several weeks to get it ready. They are told to upload the video to YouTube and share the link with me in Google Classroom. To my amazement, students put a lot of effort into adding sound effects, credits, and they even include the bloopers.

Animations. Everyone has seen a cartoon on TV. That's an animation. It takes time to get to know the software and get the timing of the characters just right, but the final product is great. I like Powtoon.

Students can publish their animation to the education section of their web page. They can also easily share the animation with a web link. There's a Chrome app for it. Here's a

student example:

Another option is Blabberize, blabberize.com.

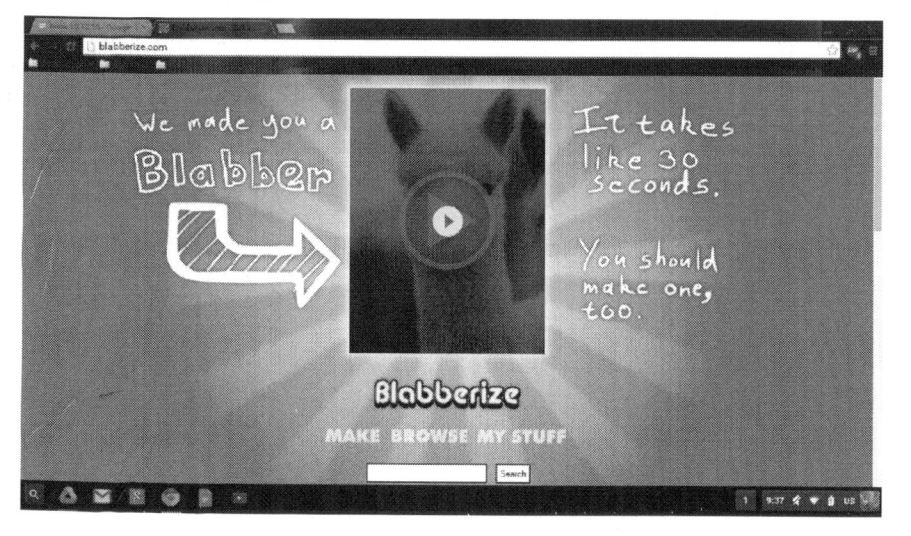

Study aids. As you can imagine, my class has a lot of vocabulary in it. Here are some tools that you can use to have students practice vocabulary: classtools.net

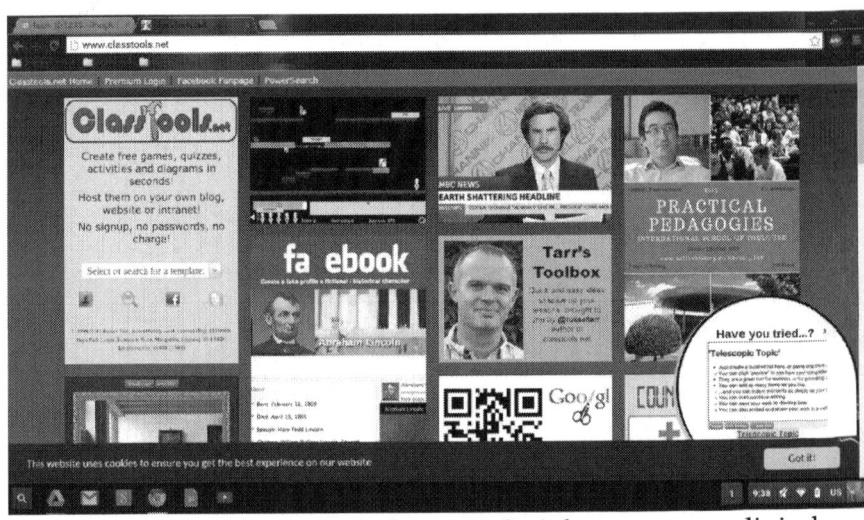

and purposegames.com. I also use Quizlet to create digital

flashcards and play games with it.

See the red Sign-in with the Google Button on the left? I suggest you use that option whenever possible. You probably have a lot of user names and passwords to remember. This makes it easier and quicker to sign in.

8 CREATING WORLD-WIDE AWARENESS

The Internet has allowed us the power to share information and ideas on a global scale. Why not take advantage that? Why not give our students a voice? Why not make real life connections?

When we allow students to share their thoughts and opinions with the world, something wonderful happens, students start to care about the quality of their work. As Rushton Hurley said, "If students are sharing their work with the world, they want it to be good. If they're just sharing it with the teacher, they want it to be good enough." This is an opportunity that we as educators can use to help achieve a higher quality of work than was possible before. Imagine Suzie writing her essay on global warming. She's only concerned with what she needs to do to get a good grade on the assignment. Once the teacher is done reading and grading it, it goes back to Suzie. She looks at it and throws it away. However, if Suzie was writing for a global audience she would be more concerned about the quality of her work because the audience is no longer limited to just the teacher, now anyone can see it. Even that boy she likes who's in her social studies class.

Twitter is a great place to connect with other teachers in your subject area and grade level. This professional learning network (PLN) is very welcoming and willing to help one another. I've found the teachers to be very friendly and encouraging.

To sign-up for a Twitter account, go to https://twitter.com/signup. Follow the instructions to set-up an account. When picking a user name, keep in mind that it's the name people will use to refer to you and connect with you in mentions, retweets, and direct messages. It will start with @ followed by the user name you chose. Your user name will also need to be less than 15 characters and not already taken by someone else. If someone asks you what your Twitter handle is, they want to know what your user name is. Give them the @_____ that you chose.

Next, edit your profile. Twitter will assign an egg as your default picture. Change that picture to a head shot of yourself. Fill out your bio. Include info about yourself that will help others of similar interests find you. For example, you can say the level you teach, the subjects, and other interests, such as gifted students, English Learners (EL), special needs, etc. Include your blog web address, if you have one. You don't need to include the name of your school if you don't want to. Some people include the verbiage "all tweets are my own." This helps prevent liability of the school or district. Putting the city and state you are from helps you to connect with other local teachers.

What's a hashtag? What does it do? A hashtag is a word that is preceded by the # symbol. It is used to help people find and follow other people who have the same interests. Cybrary Man has a long list of educational hashtags on his webpage, http://cybraryman.com/edhashtags.html. Typically a tweet has one to two hashtags. You don't want to put too many.

What's the difference between followers, following, and favorites? A follower is someone who wants to see all of your tweets. If someone follows you, you should follow them back. Typically, if this doesn't happen, the person will probably unfollow you. Favorites are often used as a way to say, I agree or I like what you said. If you want your followers to also see the tweet, you can retweet it. Whenever you retweet or favorite someone else's tweet, that person will receive a notification.

So now you have a Twitter account, now what? Start following other people who are talking about things that interest you. How do you find these people? One way is to search for a key term in the search box on the top right

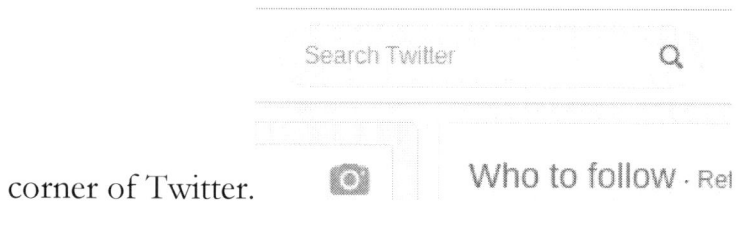

corner of Twitter.

For example, if I type math, I will see all the tweets that have recently been posted with the word math in it.

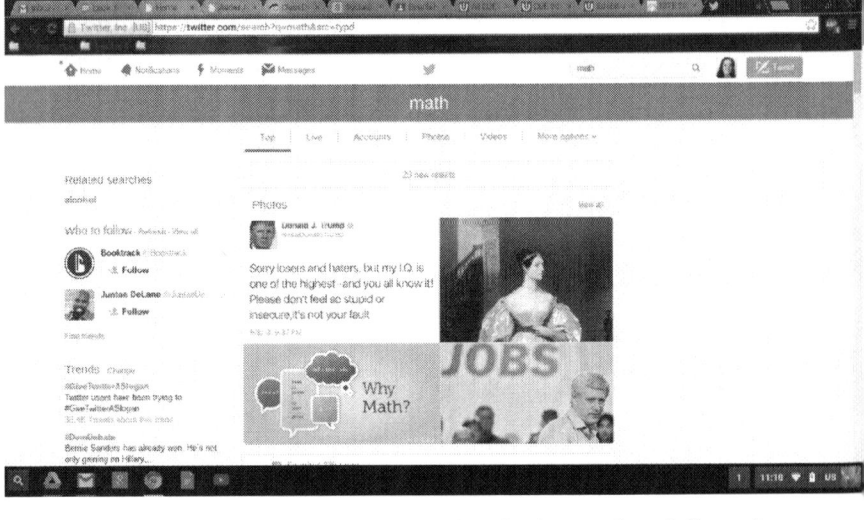

To follow someone, simply click on the follow button.

It will turn from white to blue. Another option is to get involved in Twitter chats. There are a variety of Twitter chats that take place every week about a variety of topics in education. They are a good way to meet other people and learn something new. There's usually a pre-established set of questions. You respond to the question by putting A for answer and the number of the question, for example, A1 would be your answer to number 1. You also need to end the tweet with the hashtag of the chat, like #edchat. For example: A1: (Your response to the question)#edchat.

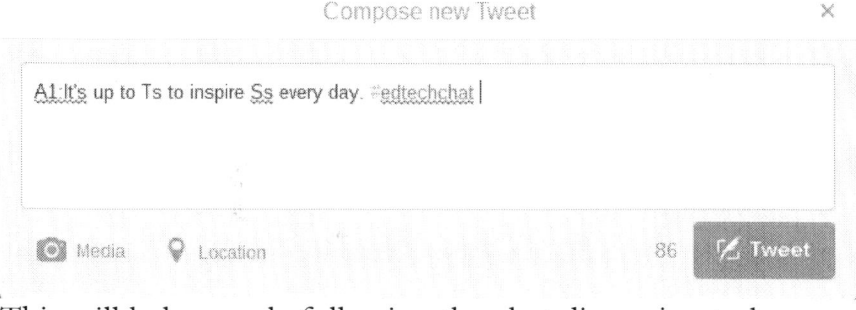

This will help people following the chat discussion to know what question you were referring to and help everyone keep track of the conversation. I warn you that some chats have a lot of participants. In these cases, it seems like the tweets fly by. It might seem overwhelming at first, but you get used to it. You don't need to respond to everything you see. Maybe the first time you just introduce yourself and favorite or retweet tweets you like. That's fine! The link to the schedule of educational twitter chats is provided in the references.

Tweets are limited to 140 characters. This is why you will see a lot of abbreviations. Some common ones you will see in our field are: Ts (teachers), Ss (students), tk (thank you), and FF (Follow Friday).

You can create a class Twitter account. Some teachers do this as a way to safeguard what the students are saying and doing with Twitter. I know a 2nd grade math teacher who connected with another 2nd grade math teacher from another state. Once a week the teachers take turns posting a math problem on Twitter for the students to respond to and interact with one another.

There are a few things to consider while using Twitter as a Professional Learning Network (PLN):

- If a teacher, librarian, principal, assistant principal, follows you, follow them back.
- If a retired or pre-service teacher follows you, follow them back.
- Don't limit yourself to just following educators in your subject area or grade level. I've taught every grade level PK-12 and college. From experience, I can tell you

that you can learn a new approach, a new idea from other subject areas and grade levels.

- Participate in Follow Friday #FF. Pick a group of educators who are new to twitter, need more followers, ones you know, ones you would like to know, ones you feel others would benefit from following, and mention them in a tweet.
- Compliments go a long way. If you like what someone is doing on Twitter, say it!
- Be positive and encouraging to others.
- Participate in #pedagoofriday . Take a photo of an activity that worked well for you and share it on Fridays. Search for #pedagoofriday every Friday to see all the wonderful lesson ideas teachers all over the world are sharing.

Skype is also a good means of communication. It's a free service that allows you to video call another person. You can communicate with people from all over the world. Skype in the Classroom provides a way for teachers to connect and have their classes communicate. If you are a German teacher, maybe you want to connect with a class in Germany and have the students ask each other questions. You can also use Skype to contact professionals around the world. For example, maybe you are learning about marine life in biology. Contact a marine biologist and do a Skype call with him/her, allowing the students a firsthand opportunity to learn what their job is all about. The possibilities are endless. However, Skype will not work on a Chromebook since it requires downloading software onto the device. I suggest using a pc and testing it out before the video call.

Google Plus is another alternative to Skype. You can find communities within Google Plus that relate to your interests. Some of the teachers there have created a Mystery Hangout. Teachers connect and pre-arrange a hangout. Students in each of the classes are connected in a video call. Students take turns asking each other questions, trying to guess where in the world the other class is located. It is like a

21st century version of Carmen Sandiego, for those of you who remember that show.

Do you remember Flat Stanley? Similar to that is the Save the Rhinos Project. Teachers sign up their class. A rhino plush is mailed to the class. Students learn about rhinos and use technology to learn and educate the world about the rhinos. The plush is then sent to another class and the process continues.

Allow your students the opportunity to share their work with the world. Let them learn from other cultures and other people. Use the resources available today with technology to empower students to make global connections.

9 ADDITIONAL NOTES

I want you to know that you're not alone in this journey. It can be a scary journey or an exciting one. It all depends on how you look at it.

Please feel free to reach out to tell me about your journey of teaching in a Chromebook Classroom. I'm also here to provide you with support, if you need it.

My blog: www.barbarasweet.com
Twitter @bsweet321

REFERENCES

Educational Twitter Chats
https://sites.google.com/site/twittereducationchats/educati
on-chat-calendar

Mystery Hangout
https://plus.google.com/communities/11036912014193535
8658

SAMR Approaches to Implementation
http://hippasus.com/rrpweblog/archives/2015/04/SAMR_
ApproachesToImplementation.pdf

Save the Rhinos Project
http://saveourrhinos.wikispaces.com/HOME

Skype in the Classroom https://education.skype.com/

Twitter 101 http://www.edudemic.com/twitter-101-a-7-
step-guide-for-teachers-newbies-and-everyone/

ABOUT THE AUTHOR

Barbara Sweet holds a Doctorate in Education in Educational Technology and e-learning, a Master's degree in Educational Technology, and a Bachelor's in Social Sciences. She is a credentialed teacher in the State of California. Her teaching experience includes PK-12th grade as well as undergraduate college students. She is passionate about education and technology.

Made in the USA
San Bernardino, CA
29 April 2016